Salmon

Salmon

hamlyn

First published in Great Britain in 2004 by

Hamlyn, a division of Octopus Publishing Group Ltd

2–4 Heron Quays, London E14 4JP

ISBN 0 600 61127 2

A CIP catalog record for this book is available from the British Library

Printed and bound in China

10 9 8 7 6 5 4 3 2 1

NOTES

1 The FDA advises that eggs should not be consumed raw. It is prudent for more vulnerable people such as pregnant and nursing mothers, invalids, the elderly, babies, and young children to avoid uncooked or lightly cooked dishes made with eggs.

2 Meat and poultry should be cooked thoroughly. To test if poultry is cooked, pierce the flesh through the thickest part with a skewer or fork—the juices should run clear, never pink or red.

3 This book includes dishes made with nuts and nut derivatives. It is advisable for those with known allergic reactions to nuts and nut derivatives and those who may be potentially vulnerable to these allergies, such as pregnant and nursing mothers, invalids, the elderly, babies, and children, to avoid dishes made with nuts and nut oils. It is also prudent to check the labels of preprepared ingredients for the possible inclusion of nut derivatives.

contents

introduction

Known as the "king of fish," salmon has a flesh that is firm, meaty, and reddish in color thanks to the pigment in its natural diet of insects and crustaceans. Quick to cook, salmon has a subtle flavor, which benefits from simple cooking methods, although its versatility allows it to be cooked in lots of different ways and with a wide variety of ingredients.

Salmon has had a mixed history, being originally a common food, then a luxury item, and back again. It is said that salmon was so common during the middle ages that apprentices living in the north of England demanded that they should not be given salmon more than three times a week! More recently, declining stocks of wild Atlantic salmon positioned the fish as a luxury food associated only with special occasions and dinner-party entertaining. However, the advent of commercial salmon farming toward the end of the 20th century changed the perception and availability of salmon once more.

While wild Atlantic salmon is now something of a scarce commodity, available only from specialist fishmarkets at a specific season and at a high price, farmed salmon is much more affordable and readily available all year round. Its increasing popularity is proved by the fact that salmon is now rated the third most popular seafood in North America. Economists tell us that as people get richer they eat more fish, and in the USA and Canada it has been shown that the average consumption of fish per head has almost doubled during the last 50 years. The current attraction of salmon lies in its flavor and nutritional properties, as well as its presentation in supermarkets in convenient ready-to-cook portions. The speed of preparing and cooking skinless, boneless fillets, for example, makes salmon ideal for a weekday family evening meal, while the lack of bones makes it even more likely to appeal to the kids!

Why fish is good for us

Current nutritional advice is that we should eat two portions of fish a week, one of which should be oil-rich fish. So, what's so great about fish?

Fish is an excellent source of protein and minerals. Its major plus point is that the protein in fish is low in saturated fat—the type of hard animal fat like beef lard, which is increasingly prevalent in our diet today and responsible for clogged arteries and heart disease. In contrast, the fat in fish takes the form of polyunsaturated

oils, a series of essential fatty acids (EFAs) that help maintain our good health. EFAs are called "essential" because they cannot be made by our own bodies and must be acquired from our diet. They include the omega-3 series of fats, which come from fish oils, and the omega-6 fats, which come from the oils in nuts, seeds, avocados, and cereal grains. Not surprisingly, oil-rich fish have the highest levels of the omega-3 fatty acids.

The health benefits of salmon

Salmon is packed with a number of important vitamins (vitamin A and various B vitamins) and minerals (calcium, copper, iron, magnesium, manganese, phosphorus, potassium, selenium, sodium, and zinc), all of which are vital for a healthy balanced diet. Above all, it is a major source of omega-3 fatty acids.

During recent years, there has been much scientific research into the numerous health benefits afforded by omega-3 fats. They have been clinically proven to help prevent coronary heart disease by reducing both cholesterol levels and high blood pressure. In addition, they have the ability, like aspirin, to make the blood less likely to clot, which helps reduce the risk of heart attacks and strokes and helps stabilize an irregular heartbeat. Furthermore, research studies have shown that omega-3 fats have a protective effect against some forms of cancer.

> ## HEALTH-GIVING PROPERTIES OF SALMON
> * Helps prevent coronary heart disease and some cancers
> * Reduces cholesterol levels and high blood pressure
> * Lowers the chances of heart attacks and strokes
> * Helps smooth irregular heartbeat
> * Boosts the immune system
> * Alleviates painful joints
> * Improves dry skin
> * Helps protect against dementia
> * Alleviates the symptoms of PMS
> * Ensures healthy growth and development of newborn babies

Fish oils are also believed to improve dry skin, help ease painful joints (especially rheumatoid arthritis), improve brain function and age-related memory loss, offer some protection against dementia (particularly Alzheimer's disease), and reduce the symptoms of PMS (premenstrual syndrome). Omega-3 fats are also necessary for the healthy growth and development of the brain and eyes of unborn and newborn babies, so pregnant and breast-feeding women should include oily fish such as salmon in their diet.

The antioxidant mineral, selenium, found in salmon, also helps protect against heart disease and the development of cancer, and helps boost the immune system generally.

In addition, canned salmon, thanks to the inclusion of edible, tender-cooked bones with the flesh, contains a significant amount of calcium, which helps strengthen our bones and fight osteoporosis.

Wild vs. farmed salmon

Salmon are migratory fish, found naturally only in the temperate and Arctic regions of the northern hemisphere—fish called "salmon" elsewhere are not true salmon. Salmon in the wild undergo a life cycle that begins with eggs being deposited by mature females in the loose gravel beds of freshwater streams. After they have hatched, the young salmon remain in the stream for a length of time dictated by water temperatures and the availability of food, after which their internal systems adapt for life in saltwater and they make their way down to the sea. After one to four years in the sea they migrate from the sea upstream usually, amazingly, to the river in which they were born, swimming against the water flow and using their ability to leap up to 10 feet (3 m) in the air to clear waterfalls. How this homing instinct works is not known. Once back at their birthplace, they spawn in the freshwater and the life cycle repeats itself.

Salmon were once abundant and fished naturally, but man's environmental incursions—among them, overfishing, global warming, pollution, and erosion of natural habitat—have inevitably resulted in dwindling wild salmon stocks. There are sustainable supplies of wild Alaskan salmon, but the stocks of wild British and Irish salmon are dangerously close to extinction. As a result, fish farming, or, aquaculture, took off in the 1980s and is now a booming industry—along the west coast of Scotland, in Norway, and Chile in particular—with the result that farmed salmon is the more usual type of salmon found on supermarket shelves. During the early 1990s, reports of cost-cutting, intensive rearing practices, and the threatened introduction of GMOs (genetically modified organisms) damaged the reputation of farmed salmon, but today good-quality, responsibly farmed conventional and organic salmon is available once more.

Farmed salmon is available from shops all year but supplies of wild salmon fluctuate. Wild Atlantic salmon is in season from summer to late fall; wild Pacific salmon from spring to fall.

SALMON TYPES

There are two main oceanic sources for salmon—the north Atlantic and northern Pacific Oceans. The Atlantic salmon *Salmo salar* is the best-known salmon (*Salmo* derives from the Latin for leaper). The Pacific salmon, which belong to the genus Oncorhynchus, include six different species—the chinook, chum (or dog), pink (or humpback), sockeye (or red), coho (or silver), and Masou salmon.

Organic salmon

Freely swimming sea fish cannot be organically certified because it is almost impossible to determine their history and living conditions. Fish like salmon, however, that can be farm-reared, *can* be organically certified. As always, the differences between organic and conventionally farmed fish include diet, living conditions, and the use of chemicals. Organic salmon farms tend to position the fish cages in strong tidal waters and to stock them less densely than conventional salmon farms. This allows the salmon to exercise and develop better muscle tone, and eliminates the need for chemical pesticides to control the sea lice that occur in crowded conditions. The flesh of organic salmon, smoked and fresh, frequently appears paler than conventionally farmed salmon (and to some people unfamiliar with its natural color rather less appealing) because of the lack of artificial coloring in their diet—the salmon are fed on crushed shrimp shells rather than additives designed to color the flesh pink.

Smoked salmon

There are two methods of smoking salmon—hot and cold smoking. Smoking was originally a highly effective way of curing freshly caught raw fish to prevent it from spoiling. Nowadays, it is the appealing smoky flavor of the fish rather than its preservation that is the reason for smoking salmon. Good smoked salmon depends very much on the quality of the original raw fish. It should be glossy and moist with a consistent color. This can vary from pale pink to reddish-brown, depending on the type and length of the smoking process. The use of different wood chips like oak, beech, and ash for the smoking process, for example, produces subtly different results. Check that the smoked salmon you are buying is well within its sell-by date. It should be soft rather than chewy with a melt-in-the-mouth texture and a strong smoky flavor.

An alternative to traditional smoked salmon is hot-smoked salmon, which has a flaky texture. The hot-smoking

process involves smoking the salmon at a much higher temperature than normal, which cooks as well as flavors the fish.

Smoked salmon has many uses. Its flavor can suffer if it is overheated so it is usually a last-minute addition to cooked dishes such as scrambled eggs (see page 44), pasta (see page 66), and risotto (see page 122). Vacuum-packed ready-sliced smoked salmon comes with thin sheets of plastic interleaved between the slices of salmon to make it easier for the cook to separate them. For recipes that require chopped or strips of smoked salmon, it is more economical to buy smoked salmon pieces or "trimmings" from the delicatessen.

The classic way to serve smoked salmon is with thinly sliced brown bread and butter, accompanied by a squeeze of lemon juice and freshly ground black pepper or cayenne pepper. Serve the smoked salmon slightly chilled; it will sweat and become oily as it warms up. Equally good, and with as many devotées, is New York-style smoked salmon, in a bagel with cream cheese.

Left, salmon fillets and, *right*, salmon steaks—both readily available all the year round in fishmarkets and grocery stores.

Buying salmon

Fresh salmon is sold whole, filleted, or in steaks. If you are buying a whole salmon, ensure that the fish is glossy-looking with bulging bright eyes and pale pink gills. The flesh should be firm and springy to the touch with little or no smell, and the gut cavity, which can harbor bacteria, should be clean. Allow for about 11½–13 oz (350–400 g) raw weight per serving when buying a whole fish with its head on.

Steaks and fillets are the cuts of salmon most commonly encountered at the supermarket. Salmon portions should also be firm and bright, rather than dull-looking, again with no "fishy" smell. Others that you are more likely to come across on restaurant menus include darnes, escalopes, and medallions.

Fillets, skinned or unskinned, are probably the most popular cuts of salmon as they contain few or no bones. Allow 4–6 oz (125–175 g) raw fillet per person for a main course, 3–4 oz (75–125 g) for an appetizer. Salmon steaks are formed by cutting across the thick part of a whole gutted salmon. Horseshoe in shape, they have a short section of backbone in the center of the steak and a band of skin around the sides.

A darne of salmon is a steak cut across the whole fish. Escalopes are thickly sliced pieces of salmon with a strip of skin on one side, while medallions are small skinless chunks of salmon.

The quality of salmon can be determined by the number of white streaks across the flesh. These streaks are layers of fat, which are clearly visible between the layers of meat and demonstrate the amount of exercise the fish had. Wild or good-quality farmed salmon have developed good muscle tone from swimming against the current and have firmer flesh with fewer fat lines, whereas poorer-quality farmed fish are caged in bays and lochs with little tidal flow and tend to be fattier with softer, gaping flesh.

Storing salmon

Store fresh or smoked salmon in the refrigerator, covered in plastic wrap or in a sealed airtight plastic container. Fresh fish is very perishable and begins to deteriorate as soon as it leaves the water. Whole fish will keep better than steaks or fillets, but it is always best on the day of purchase and must be kept refrigerated until cooked. Try not to keep fresh fish for more than 24 hours, certainly no more than 48 hours.

Salmon—raw, cooked, and smoked—freezes well, but, as with many foods, its flavor will deteriorate over time and it should not be frozen for longer than three months. Defrost thoroughly in the refrigerator before use and never refreeze fish that has been previously frozen. Fresh salmon can be frozen whole (but must be well cleaned and gutted first) or as portions. Use several layers of plastic wrap to ensure the fish is well wrapped, otherwise its texture will suffer. Dull white patches on frozen fish indicate freezer burn.

Freeze wrapped smoked salmon on the day of purchase and use within one month; vacuum-packed smoked salmon can be frozen for two to three months.

Cooking a whole salmon

If you have bought a whole salmon, it will already have been gutted.

DID YOU KNOW...?

• A fish-rich diet is good for our cardiac health and increases life expectancy. The Japanese, for example, have one of the highest rates of fish consumption, and experience the lowest level of heart disease in the industrialized world.

• Salmon trout (*Salmo trutta*), also known as sea trout or brown trout, looks like a small salmon but has more delicate flesh. It can be cooked in much the same way as salmon.

• Very fresh, good-quality salmon may be eaten raw, and is popular with lovers of Japanese food as an ingredient of sashimi.

• Where a recipe calls for cooked flaked salmon, a 6-oz (175-g) salmon steak will produce about 3½ oz (100 g) of fish once it has been cooked and the skin and bones discarded.

• To cut cooked salmon into slices or strips, refrigerating or briefly freezing the fish first will firm up the flesh and enable you to cut it cleanly.

• Salmon portions marinate well. Simply place the salmon in a shallow dish, pour over your chosen marinade—lemon juice, ginger, scallions, or soy sauce all work well—and leave to marinate overnight before cooking.

• The flakes of salmon are blocks of muscle tissue, which contract along the length of the fish and allow it to swim.

• Plainly cooked salmon is delicious served warm with a hollandaise or similar sauce, or served cold with mayonnaise or grated horseradish mixed with whipped cream.

• The quality of fresh and smoked salmon varies greatly. You really do get what you pay for, so it is worth splashing out a little more for a better flavor and texture.

• Salmon varies in fatness. Among Pacific salmon, chinook is the fattiest, coho and sockeye are somewhat less fatty, while pink and chum are lean.

However, rinse the fish under running water before use to wash away any stray scales or bones. Pat it dry inside and out with paper towels. Whole salmon is best poached in liquid in a fish kettle (see page 16)—on the stove (see page 14) or in the oven—or baked in the oven (see page 14). If you are baking it uncovered, stuff the cleaned cavity to keep the fish moist and baste it regularly. Alternatively, bake the whole salmon with fresh herbs, lemon slices, and salt and pepper in a sealed parcel of oiled foil or waxed paper so that it cooks in its own juices. A whole salmon may also be barbecued, loosely wrapped in heavyweight aluminum foil, or you can purchase a special fish basket for barbecuing a whole salmon. A ring on the handle keeps the two halves of the basket together, enclosed around the whole fish. Slide the ring down and the two halves open up like a book.

To test if the salmon is cooked, press the flesh gently with a knife—the fish should flake easily and the flakes should be evenly colored.

Cooking salmon portions

Salmon is suitable for a number of different cooking methods—many of them healthy ones requiring no extra oil—and is equally delicious served hot or cold. The main rule is to avoid overcooking the fish as the flesh can dry out—if in doubt it is best to slightly undercook your salmon, leaving the flesh still a little rosy inside.

Do not wash salmon portions before cooking as you will wash away some of their tasty juices—simply pat them dry with paper towels.

Under the broiler—Thick salmon steaks and fillets cook well under the broiler, where the intense heat seals in the flavor. Brush the fish with a little olive oil or melted butter and place in a foil-lined broiler pan. Cook under a medium to hot preheated broiler for 3–5 minutes on each side.

In the oven—Drizzle a little olive oil over salmon fillets or steaks, season with salt and pepper, and bake on an oiled cookie sheet in a preheated oven at 400°F for about 10 minutes. Alternatively, cook them in individual parcels of sealed foil, with or without the drizzle of oil or some herb-flavored butter, to retain their juices.

On the stove—Panfrying salmon fillets or steaks is quick and easy. Simply heat a little oil and butter and cook the fish for 3–4 minutes on each side—and a little longer for thicker cuts. Finish with herbs—dill is a good choice—and crème fraîche. (Make you own using equal parts whipping and sour cream.)

SALMON "CAVIAR"

Long regarded as a luxury food, caviar is traditionally the salted eggs, known as roe, of the sturgeon fish. The edible eggs of other fish such as lumpfish, herring, and salmon are also sometimes misleadingly referred to as "caviar." The correct term for salmon roe is in fact keta. Orange-red in color and the size of small peas, salmon eggs pop when eaten with a burst of strong salmony flavor. Good-quality keta is comparable with true caviar and should be served in the same way—well chilled, straight from the refrigerator, accompanied by blinis or thinly sliced toast and sour cream, along with chilled vodka or Champagne. Keta comes in jars or cans—once opened, use within three to four days.

Poaching is ideal for salmon fillets and results in moist, tender flesh. Place the fillets in a large shallow saucepan and pour in enough liquid such as milk, water, fish stock, court-bouillon (see page 22), wine, or hard cider to cover. Heat gently. Keeping the liquid just below simmering point, poach the salmon on the stove or in the oven until just done—about 10 minutes. If the salmon is to be served cold, leave it to cool in the poaching liquid to keep the flesh moist and flavorsome. Use the poaching liquid as the base for an accompanying sauce.

Steaming is another healthy cooking method that requires no butter or oil, and is ideal for salmon fillets. There are a number of different ways of steaming—just make sure the fish does not come into contact with the water, and that the pan does not boil dry. You can use a simple fold-out metal or plastic "fan" that stands in a saucepan of boiling water, the steamer rack of a wok, a Chinese bamboo steamer, or an electric steamer. Alternatively, simply place the fish between two plates set over a saucepan of boiling water. Steam the portions just as they are for about 10 minutes, or season with salt and pepper and wrap them in parcels of foil or waxed paper with thinly sliced vegetables.

Griddling, also known as chargrilling, is another way to cook salmon fillets and steaks and gives the fish a smoky flavor reminiscent of the barbecue. Drizzle a little oil over the salmon fillets, place them on the preheated hot griddle, and leave undisturbed for 2–3 minutes before rotating the portions and cooking for another 2 minutes to give criss-cross stripes. Turn the fish over and cook the other side in the same way.

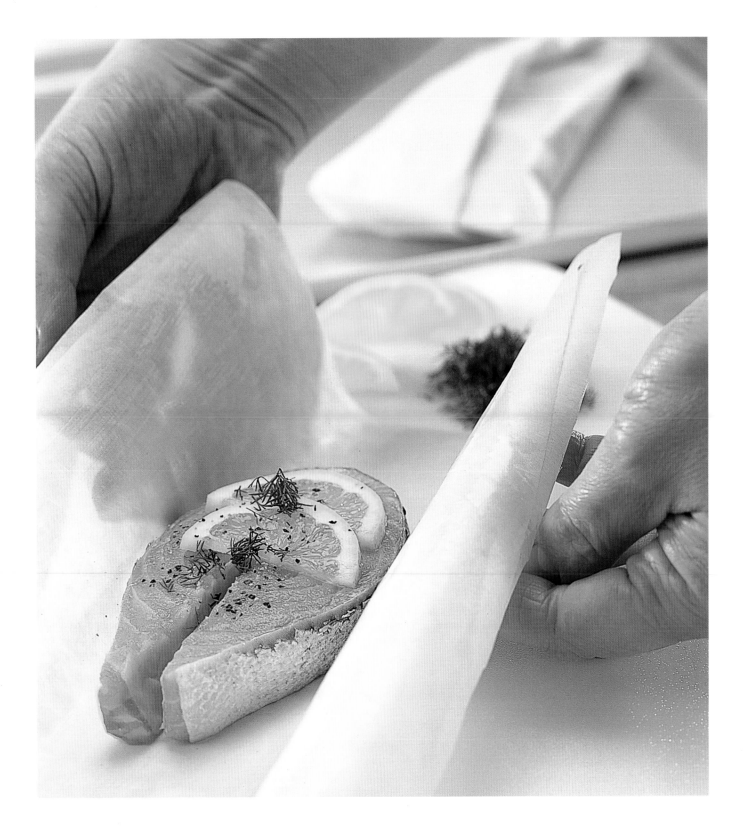

CANNED SALMON

Canned salmon is a convenient ingredient for salads, sandwiches, quiches, fish cakes, soups, and mousses. It tastes quite different from fresh salmon and the bones, which have been softened during the canning process, are edible. Of the two varieties of canned salmon available—pink and red—red salmon has the better flavor, color, and texture. Opt for salmon packed in brine rather than oil since draining water-packed salmon has little effect on the omega-3 fatty acids in the fish whereas the process of draining oil-packed salmon leaches away up to one-quarter of the desirable fats. Once a can has been opened, transfer any leftover salmon to a plastic container with a lid, refrigerate, and use within 24 hours.

In the microwave—This is a fast and effective way to cook smaller cuts of salmon. The moist atmosphere engendered by microwave cooking cooks salmon quickly, locking in its delicate flavor and all the nutrients. The steaks or fillets must all be of a similar size—arrange the pieces in a non-metallic dish with the thickest parts facing outward. The cooking time will depend on the power of your microwave and the thickness and quantity of the fish—refer to your manual for cooking guidelines. Remove the salmon from the microwave when slightly undercooked and still pink in the center, then let stand for 3–5 minutes, as it will carry on cooking.

On the barbecue—Brush the salmon portions with a little oil or butter to stop them from sticking, then season with salt and pepper. Wrap loosely in heavy foil and cook for 2–3 minutes on each side. Alternatively, use a flat wire basket specially designed for the barbecue, which holds the pieces of fish and stops them from breaking up when you turn them over. For kebabs use chunks of salmon with the skin on to help prevent the pieces from disintegrating.

Fish cooking equipment

Other than perhaps a good metal spatula for lifting the cooked fish, you do not need any specialist equipment for cooking with fish unless you intend to regularly gut, skin, and fillet your own fresh fish.

Filleting knife—A sharp knife is a prerequisite for gutting and filleting fish. A dedicated filleting knife has a thin and flexible blade, which lets you cut very close to the backbone of the fish and minimize waste. Other useful pieces of equipment include a filleting glove to protect your hands and a fish scaler, although fish scales can be removed with a blunt knife edge.

Tweezers and scissors—Fish tweezers are useful for pulling out small bones and you need sharp kitchen scissors to cut off fins and tails.

Fish kettle—Specially designed for cooking whole fish, a fish kettle is a long, deep pan with handles at each end for lifting, an inside rack on which to lay the fish, and a close-fitting lid. It is designed to cook a whole salmon in the minimum amount of liquid. If you intend to cook whole salmon regularly you might like to buy your own fish kettle, but a good supermarket or fishmarket will often lend you one.

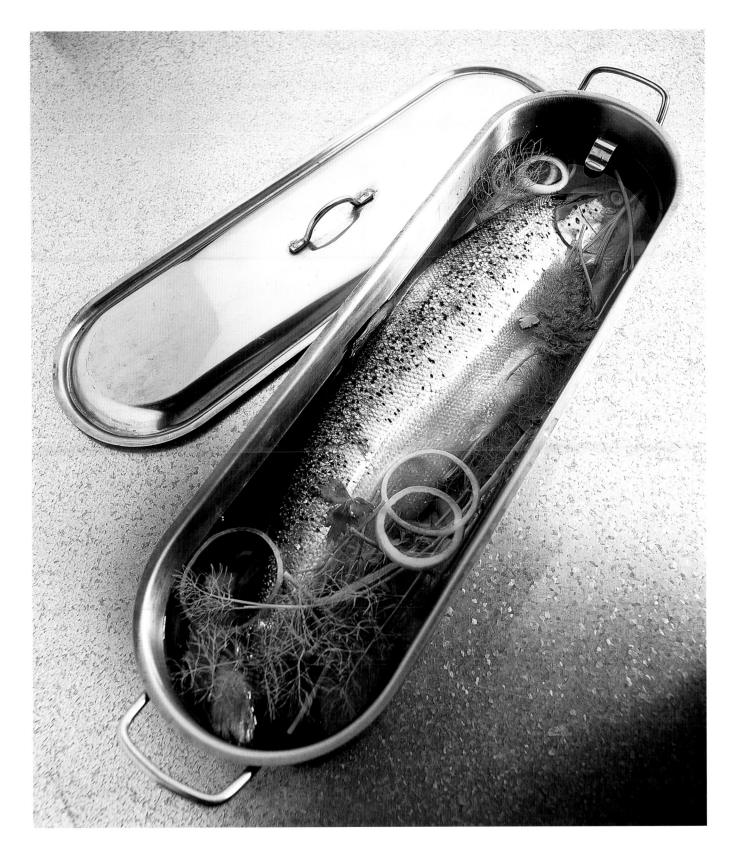

basic recipes

These are some basic recipes that appear regularly throughout the book as part of another dish, such as fish stock, or recipes that are familiar accompaniments to fish.

fish stock

2 lb/1 kg fish trimmings (see right)
3¾ cups/900 ml cold water
3¾ cups/900 ml dry white wine
3 tablespoons white wine vinegar
2 large carrots, roughly chopped
1 onion, roughly chopped
2 celery stalks, roughly chopped
2 leeks, roughly chopped
2 garlic cloves, roughly chopped
2 bay leaves
4 parsley sprigs
4 thyme sprigs
6 white peppercorns
1 teaspoon sea salt

This recipe for fish stock is the basic court-bouillon recipe with the addition of fish trimmings, plus extra wine and water. A good fish stock is important for making the basis of a soup, stew, or sauce.

Most fishmarkets will either give you any spare trimmings they have or sell them very cheaply. You can also buy freshly made fish stock from some supermarkets or use high quality fish stock cubes. Otherwise use vegetable stock cubes to make vegetable stock.

1 Wash the fish trimmings several times under cold running water and pat dry. Place in a large saucepan and add the remaining ingredients. Bring to a boil, skim the surface to remove any scum, cover, and simmer for 30 minutes.

2 Strain the liquid through a fine sieve into a clean saucepan, return to a boil, and simmer fast, uncovered, until the stock is reduced to 3 cups/900 ml. Leave to go cold and use as required.

3 This stock will keep for up to 3 days in the refrigerator or can be kept frozen in an airtight container for up to 1 month.

MAKES: about 3¾ cups/900 ml **PREPARATION TIME:** 20 minutes, plus cooling
COOKING TIME: 1 hour

anchovy butter

½ cup/125 g unsalted butter, softened

4 canned anchovy fillets in oil, drained and roughly chopped

a squeeze of lemon juice

pepper

This tasty butter, flavored with chopped anchovies, is delicious on broiled fish, as a pizza topping, or stirred into freshly cooked pasta.

1 Place all the ingredients in a food processor or blender and blend until smooth. Transfer to a bowl, cover, and store in the refrigerator for up to 1 week. Alternatively, roll the butter into a log shape, cover in plastic wrap, and freeze for up to 1 month.

MAKES: ⅔ cup/150 g **PREPARATION TIME:** 5 minutes

scordalia

1 large cooked potato (weighing about 8 oz/250 g), drained

4 garlic cloves, crushed

½ teaspoon salt

1 tablespoon lemon zest

1 tablespoon lemon juice

⅔ cup/150 ml extra virgin olive oil

pepper

This Greek garlic sauce is frequently served with poached or fried fish.

1 Place the potatoes in a bowl and mash. Stir in the garlic, salt, lemon zest, and juice. Whisk in the oil a little at a time until light and fluffy. Adjust the seasoning to taste and add a little more lemon juice if necessary. Cover and store in the refrigerator for up to 3 days.

MAKES: 12 oz/375 g **PREPARATION TIME:** 15 minutes

mayonnaise

2 egg yolks
a pinch of sugar
2 teaspoons mustard powder
2 teaspoons white wine vinegar or
   lemon juice
¼ teaspoon sea salt
1¼ cups/300 ml light olive oil
pepper

This is the basic mayonnaise recipe to which herbs, lemon, anchovies, and capers can be added. Mayonnaise is particularly good served with cold fish dishes and poached fish. If you are worried about making home-made mayonnaise then buy a high quality, ready-made mayonnaise and add flavorings to that.

1 Place the egg yolks, sugar, mustard powder, vinegar or lemon juice, salt, and a little pepper in a food processor or blender and blend for 30 seconds. With the motor running pour in the oil through the feeder tube in a steady stream until the sauce is thick and glossy.

2 If the mayonnaise is too thick, add 1–2 tablespoons boiling water and blend briefly to thin the mayonnaise to the required consistency. Season with salt and pepper to taste and store in a sealed jar, in the refrigerator for up to 5 days.

MAKES: about 1¼ cups/300 ml **PREPARATION TIME:** 10 minutes

aïoli

4–6 garlic cloves, crushed
½ teaspoon salt
2 egg yolks
1 tablespoon lemon juice
1¼ cups/300 ml light olive oil
pepper

This is the Provençal version of mayonnaise which is traditionally highly flavored with garlic. Reduce the quantity if you prefer a milder taste, although all garlic lovers will enjoy this as it is.

1 Place the garlic, salt, egg yolks, and lemon juice in a food processor or blender and blend for 1 minute. With the motor running pour in the oil through the feeder tube in a steady stream until the sauce is thick and glossy. Thin down with a little boiling water if necessary, season with salt and pepper to taste.

2 Cover and store in the refrigerator for up to 5 days.

MAKES: about 1¼ cups/300 ml **PREPARATION TIME:** 10 minutes

court-bouillon

3³/₄ cups/900 ml cold water
3³/₄ cups/900 ml dry white wine
3 tablespoons white wine vinegar
2 large carrots, roughly chopped
1 onion, roughly chopped
2 celery stalks, roughly chopped
2 leeks, roughly chopped
2 garlic cloves, roughly chopped
2 bay leaves
4 parsley sprigs
4 thyme sprigs
6 white peppercorns
1 teaspoon sea salt

This is a liquid used to poach both whole fish as well as steaks and fillets. It can be made in advance and stored in the refrigerator for 2–3 days or can be frozen for up to 1 month.

1 Place all the ingredients in a large saucepan, bring slowly to a boil, cover, and simmer for 30 minutes.

2 Strain the liquid through a fine sieve into a clean saucepan. Return to a boil and simmer fast, uncovered, for 15–20 minutes or until reduced by half. You will be left with about 2½ cups/600 ml liquid. Leave the stock to go cold and use as required.

MAKES: about 2½ cups/600 ml **PREPARATION TIME:** 15 minutes
COOKING TIME: 1 hour

olive paste

1 cup/125 g pitted black olives

2 garlic cloves, crushed

2 tablespoons/25 g capers, drained and washed

2 canned anchovy fillets in oil, drained and chopped

1 tablespoon chopped parsley

1 teaspoon chopped thyme

a pinch of mustard powder

2 tablespoons extra virgin olive oil

pepper

This delicious puree of olives, anchovies, and capers provides a tasty spread for toast and pizzas, as well as a sauce to go with broiled fish. If you have the time, use Greek kalamata olives, as they have a lovely soft flesh, and pit your own. You will need about twice the given weight of olives.

1 Place all the ingredients except the oil in a food processor or blender and puree to form a fairly smooth paste. Transfer to a jar, stir in the oil, and seal. This olive paste will keep in the refrigerator for up to 1 week. Use as required.

MAKES: about 1⅓ cups/5 oz **PREPARATION TIME:** 10 minutes

1 Soups, Snacks, and Appetizers

mediterranean salmon soup with **rouille**

1 tablespoon olive oil

2 tablespoons/25 g butter

1 onion, minced

1 carrot, finely diced

1 potato, weighing no more than 7 oz /200 g, diced

1 garlic clove, minced

1 teaspoon paprika

2 large pinches of saffron strands

2 tomatoes, skinned and diced

1 tablespoon tomato paste

3¾ cups/900 ml fish stock

½ cup/125 ml dry white wine

2 salmon steaks, weighing about 7 oz/200 g each

⅔ cup/150 ml milk

⅔ cup/150 ml light cream

salt and pepper

Rouille

1 large mild red chili, seeded and chopped

1 garlic clove, minced

3 tablespoons mayonnaise

1 small baguette, cut into 12 slices

a little paprika, for sprinkling

Although salmon is found in more northern waters, it adapts very well to this Mediterranean-style soup/stew. Rouille is the classic accompaniment. It can be very fiery but this is a mild version.

1 Heat the oil and butter in a large saucepan, add the onion, and fry gently for 5 minutes, stirring occasionally, until softened. Add the carrot and potato and fry for 5 minutes.

2 Stir in the garlic, paprika, saffron, and tomatoes and cook for 1 minute. Add the tomato paste, stock, and wine. Lower the salmon steaks into the stock and season generously with salt and pepper. Bring the stock to a boil, then reduce the heat, cover the saucepan, and simmer for 10–12 minutes, or until the salmon flakes easily when pressed lightly with a knife.

3 Lift the salmon out of the saucepan, flake it into pieces using a knife and fork, and discard the skin and bones. Reserve one-quarter of the salmon for garnish, then return the rest to the saucepan and stir in the milk and cream. Puree the soup in a food processor or blender until smooth, in batches if necessary. Taste and adjust the seasoning if needed and reheat.

4 To make the rouille, puree the chili, garlic, and mayonnaise with a little salt and pepper in a food processor or spice mill until smooth. Toast the bread lightly and top with tiny spoonfuls of rouille. Ladle the soup into bowls, sprinkle in the reserved salmon flakes, and float the toasts on top. Sprinkle with a little extra paprika and serve at once.

thai sour salmon and noodle soup

2½ oz/65 g dried medium egg thread noodles

3 scallions

1 quart/1 liter fish stock

½ carrot, cut into matchsticks

1-inch/2.5-cm piece fresh ginger root, thinly sliced

½–1 mild red chili, seeded and finely chopped

2 small salmon steaks, weighing about 5 oz/150 g each

2 tablespoons Thai fish sauce

juice of 1 lemon

½ red bell pepper, cored, seeded, and thinly sliced

1 small bunch of cilantro

1 Put the noodles into a bowl, cover them with boiling water, and leave to soak for 5 minutes. Thinly slice the bottom two-thirds of the scallions and put them into a large saucepan. Cut the remaining green tops into very thin strips, place them in cold water, and leave until they curl.

2 Add the fish stock, carrot matchsticks, ginger root, chili, and salmon to the saucepan. Bring the stock to a boil, then reduce the heat, cover the pan, and simmer for 10 minutes or until the salmon is cooked and flakes easily when lightly pressed with a knife.

3 Lift the salmon out of the pan, put it on a plate, and flake with a knife and fork, discarding any skin and bones. Return the salmon flakes to the pan and add the fish sauce, lemon juice, red bell pepper, and drained noodles. Roughly chop some of the cilantro to give 3 tablespoons, add it to the soup, and reheat.

4 Ladle the soup into bowls and sprinkle with the drained scallion curls and some extra torn cilantro leaves, if liked.

salmon chowder
with a **puff pastry hat**

1 tablespoon sunflower oil

2 leeks, thinly sliced

2 strips of rindless Canadian bacon, diced

2 tablespoons/25 g butter

3 medium potatoes, finely diced

2½ cups/600 ml fish stock

2 bay leaves

2 salmon steaks, weighing about 7 oz/200 g each

2 cups/450 ml milk

⅔ cup/125 g frozen kernel corn, just defrosted

grated zest of 1 lemon

4 tablespoons chopped parsley

1 lb/500 g frozen puff pastry, just defrosted

salt and pepper

beaten egg, to glaze

a few coarse salt flakes

1 Heat the oil in a saucepan, add the white sliced leeks (reserving the green tops), and bacon and sauté for 5 minutes, stirring until just beginning to brown. Add the butter and potato and cook for 3 minutes.

2 Pour on the stock, add the bay leaves, and season with salt and pepper, then add the fish steaks. Bring the stock to a boil, then reduce the heat, cover the pan, and simmer for 10 minutes until the salmon is just cooked and flakes when lightly pressed with a knife.

3 Lift the salmon out of the pan onto a plate and break it into flakes with a knife and fork, discarding any skin and bones. Discard the bay leaves. Add the reserved green leek tops to the pan and cook for 3 minutes until just softened. Return the salmon to the pan and add the milk, corn, lemon zest, and parsley. Leave to cool until almost ready to serve.

4 Put six 1¼-cup (300-ml) heatproof soup bowls onto a baking pan. Roll out the puff pastry on a lightly floured surface until it is a little larger than the tops of all the dishes. Using an upturned soup bowl as a guide, cut out circles of pastry for soup lids. Cut out thin strips from the trimmings and stick them onto the edges of the upturned bowls with a little beaten egg.

5 Put the dishes back onto the baking pan and fill with chowder. Brush the strips of pastry with beaten egg and press the pastry lids in position. Cut out leaves from any remaining pastry trimmings and add to the pie tops. Brush the tops with more egg and sprinkle with the salt flakes. Bake in a preheated oven at 400°F for 20 minutes until the pastry is golden and well risen and the chowder bubbling.

smoked salmon and minted cucumber cream flans

1½ cups/175 g cucumber, peeled and finely chopped

½ cup/125 g cream cheese

4 tablespoons Mayonnaise (see page 20)

2 tablespoons chopped mint

3 oz/75 g smoked salmon trimmings, chopped

salt and pepper

Shortcrust pastry

1½ cups/200 g all-purpose flour

pinch of salt

½ cup less 1 tablespoon/100 g butter, diced

2 tablespoons cold water

To garnish

cucumber slices

mint sprigs

Cucumber is one of the classic accompaniments to cold salmon. Here it is used to flavor individual smoked salmon flans—a lovely dish for a hot summer day.

1 To make the shortcrust pastry, sift the flour and salt into a bowl. Using a pastry blender, cut the butter into the flour until the mixture resembles fine breadcrumbs. Gradually stir in enough cold water to form a dough.

2 Roll out the pastry on a lightly floured surface, and line 12 deep patty pans or small fluted tart pans. Prick the bases and bake in a preheated oven at 400°F for 15 minutes or until the pastry is golden brown and crisp. Leave to cool.

3 Meanwhile, place the chopped cucumber in a colander and leave to drain for 30 minutes.

4 Beat together the cream cheese and mayonnaise until smooth, then stir in the mint, cucumber, and smoked salmon. Season with salt and pepper to taste.

5 Spoon the filling into the cooled pastry cases and level the tops. Garnish with cucumber slices and mint sprigs and serve cold.

crackling fish
pockets

1 garlic clove, crushed

½-inch/1-cm piece fresh ginger root, grated

2 tablespoons finely chopped mint

1 tablespoon sweet chili sauce

8 oz/250 g skinless salmon fillet

12 small ready-made rice flour pancakes

sunflower oil, for frying

salt and pepper

Dipping sauce

2 tablespoons light soy sauce

2 tablespoons mirin

2 tablespoons water

2 tablespoons palm sugar

½ teaspoon dried chili flakes

In this Asian-style recipe, rice flour pancakes are wrapped around small fillets of spiced salmon and fried until crisp and golden.

1 Place all the sauce ingredients in a small saucepan and heat gently to dissolve the sugar. Remove from the heat and set aside to cool.

2 Meanwhile, make the spice paste. Mix together the garlic, ginger, mint, and chili sauce. Cut the salmon into 12 equal-sized pieces and coat with the paste.

3 Soak the rice flour pancakes according to the instructions on the package. Place a piece of salmon fillet on each one, dampen the edges, and fold the pancake over and around the fish.

4 Heat the oil in a skillet and fry the pockets, in batches, for 1–2 minutes on each side, or until golden and crisp. Allow to rest for a few minutes, then serve with the dipping sauce.

SERVES: 4 **PREPARATION TIME:** 20 minutes **COOKING TIME:** 6–8 minutes

sizzling salmon with chilies

1-lb/500-g piece salmon fillet
½ teaspoon crushed dried chilies
¼ teaspoon paprika
4 teaspoons olive oil
2 avocados
grated zest and juice of 1 lime
4 teaspoons chopped cilantro leaves
salt and pepper
1 lime, cut into wedges, to garnish
(optional)

1 Cut the salmon into four slices, 1 inch/2.5 cm wide. Heat a broiler pan and add the salmon slices, skin-side down, and sprinkle with chilies, paprika, and oil and season with salt and pepper. Cook the salmon slices for 6–8 minutes, turning them once or twice until evenly browned.

2 Meanwhile, cut the avocados in half, discard the pits, and scoop the flesh onto a plate. Mash with a fork then work in the lime zest and juice and a little salt and pepper. Spoon onto 4 serving plates and spread into a thin oval.

3 Check that the salmon is cooked by testing one of the strips with a knife; the fish should flake easily and be an even color. Carefully lift the salmon onto the avocado and sprinkle with the chopped cilantro. Serve with lime wedges, if liked.

smoked salmon and tarama timbales

1 tablespoon sunflower oil, for greasing

6 oz/175 g smoked salmon, thinly sliced

6 oz/175 g taramasalata

¾ cup/175 g full-fat soft cheese (farmer's cheese or ricotta)

dash of Tabasco sauce

juice of ½ lemon

pinch of cayenne pepper

To garnish
lemon slices
dill sprigs

The combination of smoked salmon and taramasalata spiked with a dash of Tabasco sauce and a pinch of cayenne pepper makes an excellent appetizer for a dinner party.

1 Oil 4 timbale molds. Line the molds with smoked salmon and chop any leftover salmon into small pieces.

2 Mix together the taramasalata, soft cheese, Tabasco sauce, lemon juice, and cayenne pepper. Add any chopped leftover salmon.

3 Divide the mixture among the prepared molds. Level the tops and chill well for 2–3 hours.

4 To serve, carefully turn the timbales out of the molds and garnish with lemon slices and dill sprigs.

buckwheat blinis with smoked salmon

¾ cup/200 ml crème fraîche

1 tablespoon chopped dill

grated zest of 1 lemon

2 scallions, sliced

7 oz/200 g smoked salmon, cut into
   small pieces

salt and pepper

lemon wedges, to serve

Blinis

1½ cups/175 g buckwheat flour

1 teaspoon baking powder

¼ teaspoon salt

2 eggs

1 cup/250 ml milk

oil, for frying

Blinis, small buckwheat flour pancakes, originated in Russia where they are enjoyed with caviar and all types of smoked and salted fish and sour cream.

1 First make the blinis. In a bowl, mix together the buckwheat flour, baking powder, and salt, and make a well in the center.

2 Break the eggs into the well and add a little of the milk. Whisk the milk and eggs together, gradually incorporating the flour to make a smooth paste. Whisk in the remaining milk and pour into a jug.

3 Mix the crème fraîche, dill, lemon zest, and scallions and season lightly to taste with pepper.

4 Heat a little oil in a large skillet over a low heat. Carefully pour some of the batter mixture into the skillet so that it spreads to a small pancake about 2½ inches/6 cm in diameter. Pour several more dollops of batter into the skillet, keeping them slightly apart. Cook for 30–45 seconds until golden on the underside, then flip over with a metal spatula and cook for 1 more minute. Drain on paper towels and keep warm while cooking the remainder.

5 Arrange the blinis on plates, spoon some of the crème fraîche mixture onto each one, and top with pieces of smoked salmon. Serve with lemon wedges.

chinese-style gravadlax
with **ginger pickled cabbage**

2 salmon fillets, weighing 8 oz/250 g each, washed and dried

1-inch/2.5-cm piece of fresh ginger root, thinly sliced then cut into strips

1 tablespoon sugar

1 tablespoon rock salt

1 tablespoon Szechuan peppercorns, roughly crushed

2 teaspoons coriander seeds, roughly crushed

6 large dill sprigs

whole-grain mustard, to serve

Ginger Pickled Cabbage

2 teaspoons sunflower oil

1 teaspoon sesame oil

1½ cups/175 g red cabbage, shredded

1 small garlic clove, crushed

2 teaspoons grated fresh ginger root

1 tablespoon medium sweet sherry

2 tablespoons rice or wine vinegar

1 tablespoon honey

1 tablespoon dark soy sauce

¼ cup/65 ml water

2 teaspoons roasted sesame seeds

salt and pepper

A delicious variation on Scandinavian gravadlax—here the thinly sliced cured salmon is served not with a dill sauce but a tangy ginger relish.

1 Place the salmon skin-side down on a flat surface. Using tweezers, carefully pull out and discard all the small bones. Place 1 fillet skin-side down in a shallow non-reactive dish (ceramic or plastic).

2 Scatter the ginger evenly over the salmon. Mix together the sugar, salt, peppercorns, and coriander seeds, and sprinkle over the fish. Arrange the dill sprigs over the spices. Place the second salmon fillet on top, skin-side up, and cover with plastic wrap. Put a very heavy weight on top of the salmon and chill for at least 48 hours and preferably up to 3 days.

3 To make the ginger pickled cabbage, heat the two oils in a skillet. Add the cabbage, garlic, and ginger, and sauté for 10 minutes. Add the sherry, vinegar, honey, soy sauce, and water. Cover the pan and simmer for 20–25 minutes until the cabbage is tender. Remove the lid and boil for about 5 minutes to reduce the liquid until thick and syrupy. Add salt and pepper to taste then allow to cool.

4 Remove the weight and plastic wrap from the salmon and carefully brush away the spices, ginger, and dill. Using a very sharp knife, cut the fish into thin slivers and serve with the ginger pickled cabbage and a spoonful of whole-grain mustard.

salmon tartare with **fennel** and **olive paste**

1 small fennel bulb, cut lengthways
  into thin slivers

½ cup /125 ml extra virgin olive oil

3 tablespoons lemon juice

1 tablespoon grated horseradish

8-oz/250-g salmon fillet, skinned and
  finely diced

1 tablespoon chopped chervil

4 teaspoons Olive Paste
  (see page 23)

salt and pepper

To garnish

lettuce leaves

chervil sprigs

Raw salmon and thinly sliced fennel make an exotic appetizer, but do ensure that the salmon is very fresh.

1 Place the fennel in a large shallow dish. Combine the olive oil with the lemon juice, horseradish, and salt and pepper, and drizzle over the fennel. Leave to marinate at room temperature for 30 minutes.

2 Just before serving, put the diced salmon into a bowl and stir in 2 tablespoons of the fennel marinade with the chervil and a little salt and pepper. Divide the salmon into 4 portions.

3 Arrange the fennel on 4 serving plates and spoon one quarter of the salmon onto each one. Top with a spoonful of olive paste and drizzle with the remaining fennel marinade. Garnish with lettuce leaves and chervil. Serve at once.

filo-wrapped salmon with a **cream sauce**

2 salmon fillets, weighing about
   7 oz/200 g each, skinned

¼ cup/50 g butter

grated zest of 1 lemon

2 scallions, finely chopped

9½-oz/280-g package chilled filo
   pastry or 8 sheets from a larger
   frozen package, defrosted

salt and pepper

thin strips of scallion, to garnish

Cream sauce

1 cup/250 ml water

½ fish stock cube

2 egg yolks

4 tablespoons dry white wine

2 tablespoons heavy cream

2 tablespoons salmon caviar

salt and pepper

Curl the scallion strips for the garnish by soaking them in cold water for 15 minutes. For a change, add finely chopped herbs to the sauce instead of salmon caviar, if you like.

1 Cut the salmon fillets into six equal-sized pieces. Steam, covered, for 4–5 minutes until just cooked and the fish flakes when pressed with a knife. Leave to cool.

2 Beat 2 tablespoons/25 g of the butter with the lemon zest and chopped scallions and season with salt and pepper. Melt the remaining butter in a small saucepan.

3 Open out the pastry and, working with just two sheets at a time, cut each one into three 6-inch/15-cm squares. (Cover the remaining pastry sheets with a tea towel to prevent them from drying out.) Brush three of the filo squares with a little melted butter then cover each with a second square of pastry and brush the tops lightly with butter. Place a piece of salmon in the center of each one and spread with lemon butter and then fold the ends over the salmon to enclose it completely and roll it up like a cigar. Put on a baking sheet. Continue until all pieces of salmon have been wrapped with pastry. Chill until ready to serve.

4 Brush the outside edges of the pastry with the remaining butter, then bake in a preheated oven at 375°F for 6–7 minutes until the pastry is golden and the salmon piping hot. Meanwhile, heat the water with the stock cube in a small saucepan for 3–4 minutes until reduced to just under ½ cup/100 ml. Put the egg yolks into a small bowl, gradually beat in the hot stock, then add the wine. Season with salt and pepper and pour back into the pan. Heat gently, stirring continuously, for 2–3 minutes until thickened, being careful not to let the sauce boil. Stir in the cream.

5 Spoon the sauce onto 4–6 serving plates. Divide the filo parcels among the plates and sprinkle the salmon caviar over the sauce. Garnish the tops of the filo with thin strips of scallion.

smoked salmon
with **scrambled eggs**

1 tablespoon/15 g butter

3 large eggs

1 tablespoon milk

1 tablespoon cream (optional)

1–1½ oz/25–40 g smoked salmon, cut
  into narrow strips

1 teaspoon finely snipped chives

1–2 slices warm buttered toast

salt and pepper

This is an ideal dish for a weekend brunch, but it must always be cooked just before eating.

1 Melt the butter in a skillet over a gentle heat until foaming.

2 Put the eggs into a bowl and mix well with a fork. Add the milk and season with salt and pepper.

3 Pour the eggs into the foaming butter. Stir continually with a wooden spoon, scraping the bottom of the skillet and bringing the eggs from the outside to the middle. The eggs are done when they form soft creamy curds and are barely set. Remove the skillet from the heat, stir in the cream, if using, salmon, and chives and pile onto the hot toast on a warm serving plate. Serve immediately.

old english potted salmon

1-lb/500-g salmon fillet
2 tablespoons chopped tarragon
4 teaspoons drained capers
grated zest of 1 lemon
2 tablespoons lemon juice
1½ cups/375 g butter
salt and pepper

1 Cut the salmon into three pieces and steam for 8–10 minutes, or until the fish flakes easily when pressed with a knife.

2 Carefully transfer the salmon to a large plate. Flake into chunky pieces with a knife and fork, discarding any skin and bones. Add the tarragon, capers, and lemon zest, then divide the mixture among six ½-cup/150-ml individual dishes.

3 Melt the butter in a saucepan, bring it just to a boil, then take it off the heat and skim off the scum with a dessertspoon. Pour the remaining butter through a fine sieve into a bowl and leave for 10 minutes to settle. Carefully spoon the clear butter out of the bowl into a clean dish, leaving behind the white sediment. Stir the lemon juice into the clear butter and season with salt and pepper.

4 Spoon the lemon butter into the individual dishes, then loosen the fish flakes with a fork so that the butter can penetrate to the bottom. Put the dishes on a cookie sheet and chill for 2–3 hours until firm. About 30–45 minutes before serving, remove the dishes from the refrigerator and allow to come to room temperature. Serve with warm crusty whole-grain bread and a watercress salad.

smoked salmon and **quails' egg** salad

1⅔ cups/250 g small new potatoes

about 8 cups/250 g packaged salad mix (such as curly endive, arugula, corn salad, batavia, or romaine)

2–3 tablespoons skillet-fried croûtons

1 teaspoon white wine vinegar

12 quails' eggs

4 oz/125 g smoked salmon, cut into strips

2 tablespoons snipped chives

salt and pepper

Dressing

5 tablespoons Mayonnaise (see page 20)

1 tablespoon lemon juice

3–4 tablespoons water

1 Boil the potatoes for about 10 minutes, or until just tender. Refresh under cold running water and drain thoroughly. Allow to cool completely, then cut the potatoes into halves or quarters.

2 To make the dressing, mix together the mayonnaise, lemon juice, and water.

3 Shortly before serving, arrange the lettuce leaves on a large shallow serving dish or on individual plates. Scatter the croutons over the top.

4 Bring a skillet of water to simmering point. Add the vinegar. Carefully break in 6 of the quails' eggs and poach for about 1 minute. Using a slotted spoon, transfer the poached eggs to a plate, and repeat with the remaining eggs. Alternatively, fry the eggs in butter until just firm.

5 Arrange the cooked quails' eggs, potatoes, and salmon strips on the salad. Sprinkle with the snipped chives and add salt and pepper to taste. Drizzle with the dressing.

ceviche of salmon

6-oz/175-g salmon fillet
lemon juice, for sprinkling
olive oil, for sprinkling
salt and pepper
dill or fennel sprigs, to garnish

Ceviche (sometimes spelled seviche) is a method of "cooking" fish by marinating it in lemon or lime juice. It originated in South America.

1 Using a sharp knife, cut down through the fillet of salmon into very thin slices—about the same thickness as sliced smoked salmon. Arrange the raw salmon on 2 plates in a single layer.

2 Sprinkle the salmon evenly with lemon juice and olive oil and season to taste with salt and pepper.

3 Garnish with dill or fennel sprigs and serve immediately with thinly sliced brown bread and butter.

2 Light Lunches

salmon with summer vegetable medley

8-oz/250-g salmon fillet, in one piece

1–1½ tablespoons cornstarch

1 tablespoon sugar

1 tablespoon dark soy sauce

1 tablespoon dry sherry

2 teaspoons white wine vinegar

1 teaspoon grated fresh ginger root

2 tablespoons sunflower oil

¼ cup/50 ml vegetable stock

1 cup/50 g baby sweetcorn, sliced lengthways

1 cup/50 g sugar snap peas, trimmed

4–6 baby carrots (about 50g), trimmed but left whole

8 fine asparagus spears (about 50 g)

2 shallots, finely chopped

salt and pepper

This dish should be cooked right at the last minute and served immediately.

1 Remove the skin from the underside of the salmon fillet. Cut the fish across into 1-inch/2.5-cm strips. Sprinkle the cornstarch onto a plate and season with salt and pepper. Add the salmon pieces and toss gently to coat them all over. Transfer the salmon to a dish.

2 Put the remaining seasoned cornstarch (there will be about 2 teaspoons) into a small bowl. Add 1 tablespoon cold water and stir until smooth. Add the sugar, soy sauce, dry sherry, vinegar, ginger root, and vegetable stock, and stir to combine.

3 Heat half the oil in a wok or skillet. Add the salmon pieces and cook, turning them gently until they are browned. Remove the salmon from the wok with a slotted spoon and keep hot. Add the remaining oil to the wok and stir in the sweetcorn, sugar snap peas, carrots, asparagus, and shallots and cook, stirring constantly, for 2–3 minutes. Add 2 tablespoons water, cover, and cook for 3–4 minutes until the vegetables are tender—shaking the wok occasionally.

4 Stir the cornstarch mixture and pour it over the vegetables in the wok. Add the salmon pieces. Turn the salmon and vegetables to coat them with the glaze as the sauce comes to a boil and thickens. Serve hot.

layered salmon
with **potato cakes**
and **watercress sauce**

1⅔ cups/425 g raw potato, grated
3–4 tablespoons olive oil
4 salmon fillets, weighing about
    4 oz/125 g each
butter, for broiling

Watercress Sauce
2–3 bunches of watercress
1¼ cups/250 ml crème fraîche
lemon juice, to taste
salt and pepper

1 First prepare the watercress sauce. Chop the watercress, reserving 4 sprigs for garnish, then put the crème fraîche, and chopped watercress into a saucepan and stir together. Add lemon juice and salt and pepper to taste and set aside.

2 Put the grated potato into a bowl and season with salt and pepper. Divide the mixture into 4 cakes. Heat the oil in a skillet, add the potato cakes and cook over a moderate heat until browned all over and softened inside. Remove from the skillet and set aside to keep warm.

3 Meanwhile, season the salmon fillets with salt and pepper. Line a broiler pan with a piece of greased foil and arrange the fillets on top. Dot with butter and cook under a preheated broiler for 4–5 minutes on each side until cooked through.

4 Heat the watercress sauce gently—it may be served cold if preferred.

5 To serve, place a potato cake on each plate, put the salmon on top, and pour the sauce over. Garnish with watercress sprigs and serve immediately.

salmon parcels
with **red bell peppers**

4 salmon steaks, about 1 inch/
  2.5 cm thick

2 tablespoons sunflower oil

2 tablespoons white wine vinegar

¼ cup/50 g butter

2 red bell peppers, cored, seeded,
  and finely sliced

2–3 tablespoons chopped dill

salt and pepper

lemon quarters, to serve

1 Arrange the salmon steaks in a single layer in a shallow dish. Mix together the oil and vinegar and season with pepper. Pour the dressing over the salmon steaks, turning to coat them on both sides. Cover and marinate for 1 hour.

2 Cut 4 squares of foil, each one large enough to enclose a salmon steak. Brush each sheet on one side with oil. Melt the butter in a skillet. Stir in the sliced red bell pepper and cook for 4–6 minutes. Stir in the dill. Lift the salmon steaks out of the marinade and put one in the center of each piece of foil. Season with salt and top with some buttered red bell peppers. Fold the foil around the fish, turning the folded ends underneath. Arrange the fish parcels in one layer on a baking pan.

3 Bake the salmon parcels in a preheated oven at 350°F for 15–20 minutes. Serve hot with lemon quarters.

salmon and chèvre soufflés

butter, for greasing

4 tablespoons freshly grated
    Parmesan cheese

2 small salmon steaks, weighing
    about 5 oz/150 g each

1¼ cups/300 ml milk

¼ cup/50 g butter

⅓ cup/50 g all-purpose flour

3½ oz/100 g chèvre cheese, diced

3 egg yolks

1 teaspoon Dijon-style mustard

2 tablespoons chopped basil, chives,
    or parsley

4 egg whites

salt and pepper

1 Butter the base and sides of two 1-quart/1.2-liter heatproof soufflé dishes, 6 inches/15 cm in diameter, then sprinkle with the Parmesan.

2 Arrange the salmon in a single layer in a saucepan or deep skillet. Pour over the milk and bring it to a boil, then cover and poach the fish for 6–8 minutes or until it flakes when lightly pressed with a knife. Carefully lift the salmon out of the milk and put it on a plate; break it into small flakes with a knife and fork, discarding the skin and any bones. Strain the milk into a measuring jug and make up to 1¼ cups/300 ml with water.

3 Melt the butter in the cleaned salmon pan, stir in the flour, then gradually blend in the milk and bring it to a boil, stirring until it is very thick and smooth. Remove the pan from the heat and beat in the chèvre. Gradually beat in the yolks, one at a time, stirring well between each addition, then stir in the mustard, herbs, and flaked salmon and season with salt and pepper.

4 Whisk the egg whites in a separate bowl until peaking. Fold one-quarter of them into the salmon mixture to loosen it, then fold in the remainder. Gently pour the mixture into the prepared soufflé dishes and bake in a preheated oven at 375°F for 25–30 minutes until the soufflés are well risen and golden and the centers are still soft but not runny. Serve immediately with a salad.

salmon, olive, and **arugula baguettine**

3 tablespoons/40 g butter

1 large red onion, thinly sliced

pinch of sugar

pinch of salt

1 teaspoon chopped thyme

2 salmon fillets, weighing about
    8 oz/250 g each, from the head
    end of the fish, skinned

2 tablespoons seasoned flour

2 tablespoons olive oil

3 tablespoons lemon juice

4 baguettine rolls

4 tablespoons Olive Paste
    (see page 23)

6 cups/125 g arugula

**This is a fish version of a steak and onion baguette and just as tasty.
A baguettine roll is the name used for a medium-sized French baguette.**

1 Melt half of the butter in a heavy skillet and fry the onion, sugar, salt, and thyme for 15 minutes until golden and caramelized. Set aside.

2 Cut each piece of salmon into ¼-inch/5-mm thick slices, cutting through at a slight angle, and dust lightly with the seasoned flour.

3 Melt the remaining butter and the oil in a nonstick skillet and, as soon as the butter stops foaming, add the salmon strips, in batches, and fry for 1 minute on each side until golden and crispy. Remove the pan from the heat and pour in the lemon juice, stirring well.

4 Slice almost through each baguettine and spread with the olive paste. Fill each one with arugula, some caramelized onion and salmon pieces, and pour over the pan juices. Serve at once.

SERVES: 4 **PREPARATION TIME:** 15 minutes **COOKING TIME:** 8–10 minutes

broiled salmon steaks with herb butter

½ cup/125 g butter, softened

2 tablespoons mixed herbs (such as parsley, dill, chervil, chives, or fennel), very finely chopped

squeeze of lemon juice

¼ cup/50 g butter, melted

4 salmon steaks, about 6–8 oz/175–250 g each (¾–1 inch/2–2.5 cm thick)

salt and pepper

To garnish

4 lemon wedges

watercress sprigs

1 Mix the butter, herbs, and lemon juice. Place on a piece of greaseproof paper and roll it into a log shape about 1 inch/2.5 cm in diameter. Chill until solid.

2 Brush a baking pan with the melted butter and place the salmon steaks on top. Brush with half of the remaining butter and season well with salt and pepper. Cook under a preheated moderate broiler for about 4–5 minutes on each side. When turning each steak, brush with more melted butter and season again. Alternatively, the steaks can be cooked on a cast-iron grill pan.

3 Cut the log of herb butter into 4 circles. Transfer the cooked steaks carefully onto warm plates and top each one with a circle of butter. Garnish with lemon wedges and watercress sprigs.

salmon and **potato parcels**

1 large potato (about 250 g), cubed

1 tablespoon/15 g butter

½ onion, finely chopped

¼ teaspoon fennel seeds, roughly ground

1 teaspoon finely grated lemon zest

1 tablespoon chopped dill

6 oz/175 g smoked salmon, finely chopped

1 tablespoon lemon juice

1 egg yolk

1 lb/500 g puff pastry, defrosted if frozen

salt and pepper

flour, for dusting

Egg glaze

1 small egg

1 tablespoon milk

pinch of salt

1 Boil the potato in lightly salted water for about 20 minutes, or until tender.

2 Meanwhile, melt the butter in a small saucepan and fry the onion, fennel seeds, and lemon zest for 10 minutes, until very soft. Transfer to a bowl.

3 Drain the cooked potato well and mash with a fork—the texture of the mashed potato should remain fairly rough. Add to the onion with the dill, smoked salmon, lemon juice, and egg yolk and mix until well blended. Season with salt and pepper.

4 Roll out the puff pastry on a lightly floured surface to form a thin rectangle, 7 x 14 inches/18 x 35 cm. Cut into 8 squares, measuring 3½ inches/8.5 cm.

5 Divide the filling among the squares, placing a mound of filling slightly off center on each one. Dampen the edges of the squares and fold each one in half diagonally to form a triangle. Press the edges together to seal.

6 Transfer the pastry triangles to a lightly greased cookie sheet. Beat together the ingredients for the egg glaze and brush the glaze lightly over the pastry. Bake in a preheated oven at 425°F for 15–20 minutes, until puffed up and golden. Serve hot.

salmon and dolcelatte tart

2 salmon steaks, weighing about 7 oz/200 g each

1 tablespoon olive oil

1 leek, thinly sliced

4 oz/125 g dolcelatte cheese, rind removed

5 eggs

⅔ cup/150 ml light cream

⅔ cup/150 ml milk

salt and pepper

Tart case

2 cups/250 g all-purpose flour

½ cup/50 g medium oatmeal

pinch of salt

⅓ cup/75 g butter

½ cup/75 g white vegetable shortening

3–3½ tablespoons cold water

1 To make the tart case, put the flour, oatmeal, and salt into a large bowl. Dice the butter and shortening and add to the bowl. Then blend in with a pastry cutter until the mixture resembles fine breadcrumbs. Stir in enough water to make a smooth dough.

2 Knead the pastry lightly on a floured surface, then roll out and line a buttered 11-inch/27-cm tart pan with a removeable bottom. Press the pastry over the base and up the sides of the pan and trim off the excess. Prick the base with a fork, then chill for 15 minutes.

3 Meanwhile, steam the salmon, covered, for 8–10 minutes or until the fish flakes when pressed with a knife. Put the salmon on a plate and flake with a knife and fork, discarding any skin and bones. Heat the oil in a skillet, add the leek and fry for 5 minutes, stirring until softened. Dice the cheese. Whisk together the eggs, cream, and milk and season with salt and pepper.

4 Put the tart case on a cookie sheet and line the tart with a large piece of waxed paper and fill with ceramic pie weights (or use dried beans or rice if you don't have any pie weights). Bake in a preheated oven at 400°F for 10 minutes. Remove the paper and beans and cook for 5 more minutes, until the edges of the tart are browned. Remove the tart from the oven and reduce the heat to 350°F.

5 Spoon the salmon flakes, leek, and cheese into the tart case. Pour in the egg mixture and return the tart to the oven for 30–35 minutes until the filling is set and golden. Allow the tart to cool for at least 30 minutes, then carefully take it out of the pan and transfer to a serving plate. Serve warm or cold with a tossed green salad.

layered salmon **terrine**

2 tablespoons cold water

2 teaspoons powdered gelatin

1 salmon fillet, weighing about
   13 oz/400 g, skinned

½ fish stock cube

2 cups/50 g watercress, finely
   chopped

grated zest of 1 lemon

1¼ cups/300 ml crème fraîche

10 oz/300 g sliced smoked salmon

salt and pepper

a few extra watercress sprigs, to
   garnish

This terrine not only tastes good, but the contrast between the salmon and watercress looks highly decorative too.

1 Put the cold water into a small bowl. Sprinkle over the gelatin, making sure all the powder is absorbed, then leave to soak for 5 minutes. Thinly slice the salmon fillet and place a single layer in a steamer. Cover and cook for 3–4 minutes until the salmon flakes when pressed with a knife. Lift the steamer top and lid off the pan and allow the salmon to cool. Cook the remaining salmon in the same way. Use ⅔ cup/150 ml water from the base of the steamer to dissolve the stock cube, then leave to cool.

2 Stir the chopped watercress and lemon zest into the crème fraîche and season with salt and pepper.

3 Put a bowl with one-third of the gelatin into a saucepan of water so that the water comes halfway up the sides of the bowl and heat for 4–5 minutes until the gelatin has dissolved and the liquid is clear. Gradually mix the dissolved gelatin and one-third of the cooled stock. Stir in one-third of the crème fraîche, then set aside.

4 Line a 2-lb/1-kg loaf pan with plastic wrap and leave the ends hanging over the pan. Separate the smoked salmon slices and use to cover the base and sides of the pan, reserving enough to cover the top of the pan when filled. Pour one-third of the crème fraîche mixture into the base of the pan and chill for 2 hours until set.

5 Arrange half the cooked salmon slices in the pan to cover the crème fraîche mixture. Melt the remaining gelatin, mix with the remaining crème fraîche mixture and stock, and leave to cool. Spread half over the salmon slices. Cover with the remaining cooked salmon, then the last of the crème fraîche mixture. Complete the terrine by covering the final crème fraîche layer with the reserved smoked salmon. Fold the ends of the plastic wrap over the smoked salmon and chill for 3–4 hours, or overnight, until firmly set.

6 To serve, unfold the top of the plastic wrap, invert the pan onto a plate, then remove the pan and plastic wrap. Cut the terrine into 8 slices and arrange on plates with watercress sprigs to garnish.

pasta with smoked salmon

3⅓ cups/300 g penne or other dried pasta shapes

1¼ cups/300 ml crème fraîche

½ cup/125 ml vodka

2 scallions, finely chopped (optional)

2 teaspoons finely chopped dill, extra for garnish

8 oz/250 g smoked salmon, cut into strips

salt and pepper

1 Cook the pasta in a large saucepan of lightly salted boiling water for 8–12 minutes until just tender.

2 When the pasta is almost ready, pour the crème fraîche and vodka into a saucepan and heat gently until almost boiling.

3 Add the scallions, if using, and dill, season with salt and pepper, and cook until heated through. Remove the pan from the heat and stir in the strips of smoked salmon.

4 Drain the pasta thoroughly and toss with the sauce. Garnish with dill sprigs and serve immediately.

panfried salmon with **tomato coulis**

1 tablespoon olive oil

1 garlic clove, crushed

2 salmon steaks or cutlets, about 6 oz/175 g each

ground nutmeg, to taste

½ small glass red wine (optional)

salt and pepper

mixed green lettuce leaves, to serve

Tomato Coulis

1½ lb/750 g ripe tomatoes, skinned and thinly sliced

1 small onion, finely chopped

dash of sugar

bouquet garni

juice of ½ lemon

salt and pepper

1 Place all the ingredients for the tomato coulis, except the lemon juice, in a saucepan and bring to a boil. Reduce the heat, cover the saucepan, and simmer for about 20 minutes until very soft. Remove the bouquet garni.

2 Puree the tomato mixture in a food processor, then press through a sieve. Return to a boil and reduce to a saucelike consistency. Add the lemon juice and season to taste with salt and pepper.

3 Heat the oil and gently fry the garlic for a few minutes, then discard the garlic. Season the salmon with salt and nutmeg. Add it to the pan and sauté over a high heat for a few seconds on each side, then reduce the heat and cook the fish for 3–5 minutes on each side until cooked through. Remove and keep warm. Deglaze the pan with the red wine and add to the coulis.

4 Place a portion of salmon on each individual plate and spoon over the tomato coulis. Serve with mixed green lettuce leaves.

warm **tea-smoked salmon salad** with **wilted arugula**

4 salmon fillets, weighing about
    4oz/125 g each
1 cup/125 g cherry tomatoes, halved
6 cups/125 g arugula

Smoke mix
8 tablespoons Jasmine tea leaves
8 tablespoons soft brown sugar
8 tablespoons long-grain rice

Dressing
1 shallot, finely chopped
1 garlic clove, minced
a few thyme leaves
1 teaspoon Dijon-style mustard
2 teaspoons white wine vinegar
4–5 tablespoons extra virgin olive oil
salt and pepper

Although smoking fish and meat over a mixture of tea leaves, sugar, and rice is a method widely used in Chinese cooking, this dish adapts the method for Western tastes. You will need a wok with a lid and a trivet for this recipe.

1 Mix together all the ingredients for the smoke mix. Line a wok with a large sheet of foil, allowing it to overhang the edges, and pour in the smoke mix. Place a trivet over the top. Cover with a tight-fitting lid and heat for 5 minutes, or until the mixture is smoking.

2 Meanwhile, remove any bones from the salmon with tweezers. Place the tomatoes in a bowl with the arugula.

3 Quickly remove the lid from the wok and place the salmon fillets, skin-side down, on the trivet. Cover and cook over a high heat for 5 minutes. Remove from the heat and set aside, covered, for another 3 minutes.

4 Meanwhile, make the dressing. Put the shallots, garlic, thyme leaves, mustard, vinegar, and oil in a bowl and season to taste with salt and pepper. Whisk thoroughly to combine.

5 Flake the salmon into the salad, add the dressing, and toss well. Serve immediately.

potato salad with smoked salmon, grapes, and pecans

2 medium-sized round white or round red waxy potatoes (about 300 g), boiled and sliced

1 oz/25 g smoked salmon, cut into thin strips

4 oz/125 g cooked shelled shrimp

½ cup/50 g seedless white grapes, halved

¼ cup/25 g pecans

1 tablespoon snipped chives

1 tablespoon chopped dill, to garnish

Dressing

1 tablespoon Mayonnaise (see page 20)

2 tablespoons sour cream

1 teaspoon lemon juice

salt and pepper

1 Put the sliced potatoes in a bowl and mix in the smoked salmon, shrimp, grapes, pecans, and chives.

2 Whisk together all the dressing ingredients in a jug.

3 Pour the dressing over the salad, toss lightly, and sprinkle with dill.

italian salmon salad

3 cups/175 g pasta bows

7-oz/200-g can salmon in brine, drained and flaked

1 red bell pepper, cored, seeded, and finely diced

½ cucumber, finely diced

12 pitted black olives

2 tablespoons Mayonnaise (see page 20)

watercress sprigs, to garnish

1 Cook the pasta in a large saucepan of lightly salted boiling water for 10–12 minutes until just tender. Drain thoroughly and leave to cool.

2 Mix the flaked salmon with the red bell pepper, cucumber, olives, and pasta. Pour over the mayonnaise and toss lightly. Arrange in a serving dish and garnish with watercress sprigs.

lasagna marinara

9 dried no-boil lasagna noodles
2 eggs
2 cups/200 g Cheddar cheese, grated
dill sprigs, to garnish

Sauce
¼ cup/50 g butter
⅓ cup/50 g all-purpose flour
2½ cups/600 ml milk
a few saffron threads
8-oz/250-g salmon tail
8-oz/250-g cod fillet
6 oz/175 g squid rings
salt and pepper

1 To make the sauce, melt the butter in a saucepan, stir in the flour, and cook for 1 minute. Gradually add the milk, whisking or beating the sauce over a moderate heat until it thickens. Crush the saffron threads to a powder in a bowl and stir in 2–3 tablespoons boiling water until dissolved. Add to the sauce with salt and pepper to taste. Mix well.

2 Remove any bones from the salmon and cod and cut the fish into bite-sized pieces. Fold into the sauce with the squid rings. Remove from the heat.

3 Spoon one-third of the fish into a 3-pint/1.75-liter ovenproof dish and cover with a layer of lasagna noodles. Repeat these layers twice, finishing with a layer of lasagna.

4 Beat the eggs and Cheddar in a bowl. Add salt and pepper to taste and pour over the lasagna. Bake in a preheated oven at 375°F for 45 minutes, covering the dish with foil after 30 minutes if the top starts to overbrown.

3 Fast and Delicious

smoked salmon and **asparagus sauce** with **fettucine**

6 oz/175 g asparagus tips

12 oz/375 g fettucine or tagliatelle

4 oz/125 g smoked salmon, cut into thin strips

1¼ cups/300 ml heavy cream

1 tablespoon chopped tarragon

salt and pepper

Parmesan cheese shavings, to garnish (optional)

1 Blanch the asparagus tips in lightly salted boiling water for 5 minutes. Drain the tips under cold running water and pat dry.

2 Meanwhile, cook the pasta in a large saucepan of lightly salted boiling water for 8–12 minutes, until just tender. Drain and return to the pan. Toss over a low heat with the asparagus, smoked salmon, cream, tarragon, and salt and pepper until heated through.

3 Transfer to a warmed serving dish and garnish with wafer-thin shavings of Parmesan cheese, if liked.

salmon roasted with fennel, vine-ripened tomatoes, and red onions

4 salmon fillets, weighing about 6–8 oz/175–250 g each

4 tablespoons lemon juice

4 tablespoons olive oil

1 tablespoon balsamic vinegar

1 tablespoon honey

4 garlic cloves, minced

2 red onions, quartered

2 fennel bulbs, quartered

16–20 vine-ripened cherry tomatoes

salt and pepper

rice or couscous, to serve

1 Season the salmon fillets generously with salt and pepper and pour the lemon juice over them. Set aside.

2 In a small bowl, combine the olive oil, balsamic vinegar, honey, and garlic, and season with salt and pepper. Put the onion, fennel, and tomatoes in a bowl and pour over the oil mixture. Toss to coat thoroughly, then spread on a baking pan. Place in a preheated oven at 425°F and roast for 10 minutes. Add the salmon fillets to the baking pan and roast for a further 12–15 minutes.

3 Remove the salmon from the oven when it is cooked through and serve with the roasted vegetables and rice or couscous.

parma ham-wrapped salmon

**4 salmon fillets, weighing
6 oz/175 g each, skinned**

**4 thin slices fontina cheese, rind
removed**

16 sage leaves

8 thin slices Parma ham

sea salt and pepper

To serve

**freshly cooked pasta tossed in
chopped parsley**

arugula leaves

1 tablespoon balsamic vinegar

1 tablespoon olive oil

1 Season the salmon fillets and trim the fontina slices to fit on top of the salmon.

2 Place a slice of fontina on top of each salmon fillet, then add 4 sage leaves. Wrap 2 pieces of Parma ham around each salmon fillet to hold the cheese and sage leaves in place.

3 Heat a griddle pan. Cook the wrapped salmon fillets for 5 minutes on each side, taking care when turning them over. Serve with freshly cooked pasta tossed in parsley and an arugula salad dressed with balsamic vinegar and olive oil.

salmon **chermoula**

6 skinless salmon steaks, cut from
  the thick end of the fillet
butter, for greasing

Chermoula
2 teaspoons cumin seeds
1 teaspoon coriander seeds
¼ teaspoon crushed dried chilies, or
  1 teaspoon mild chili seasoning
3 garlic cloves, crushed
finely grated zest and juice of 1 lime
3 tablespoons olive oil
½ cup/8 g cilantro, chopped
¼ cup/8 g flat-leaf parsley, chopped
salt

Chermoula, an aromatic herb and spice blend, is used here to envelop fish and impart an exotic flavor.

1 To make the chermoula, lightly pound the cumin and coriander seeds using a mortar and pestle (or a small bowl and the end of a rolling pin). Tip into a bowl and add the chilies or chili seasoning, garlic, lime zest and juice, oil, herbs, and a little salt.

2 Put the salmon steaks in a shallow dish, add the chermoula, and turn the fish to coat with the mixture.

3 Lightly butter a large, shallow broiler pan. Lift the salmon steaks out of the marinade, reserving the juices, and put them skinned-side up in the dish. Cook under a preheated very hot broiler for 4 minutes. Turn the salmon steaks over and spoon on the remaining marinade. Broil for a further 4 minutes or until cooked through. Serve immediately.

crushed new potatoes
with **herby salmon**

1½ lb/750 g new potatoes

pat of butter

grated zest and juice of 2 limes

1 bunch of scallions, sliced

4 pieces skinless salmon fillet,
   weighing about 4 oz/125 g each

4 tablespoons light crème fraîche

3 tablespoons chopped mixed herbs
   (such as parsley and dill)

salt and pepper

lime wedges, to garnish

1 Cook the potatoes in lightly salted boiling water for 10–15 minutes until tender. Drain and lightly crush with a fork.

2 Stir in the butter, half of the lime zest and juice, and half of the scallions and season with plenty of black pepper.

3 Meanwhile, place the salmon pieces on a foil-lined broiler pan and cook under a preheated moderate broiler for 6–7 minutes, turning them halfway through cooking, or until the fish is just cooked.

4 Mix together the remaining lime zest and juice and scallions and the crème fraîche and herbs. Serve the salmon with the potatoes and herby sauce, garnished with lime wedges.

salmon steaks
with **watercress mayonnaise**

4 salmon steaks, weighing about
   4–5 oz/125–150 g each

4 teaspoons extra virgin olive oil

juice of 1 lemon

1 bunch of watercress

4 tablespoons Mayonnaise
   (see page 20)

1 teaspoon Tabasco sauce (optional)

salt and pepper

This is an easy dish to prepare and deceptively sophisticated when served.

1 Place the salmon steaks on a foil-lined broiler pan and drizzle one teaspoon each of olive oil and lemon juice over each steak. Season with pepper and broil under a preheated medium-high heat for about 5 minutes on each side.

2 While the salmon is cooking, put the watercress, mayonnaise, and remaining lemon juice in a food processor and blend to a smooth sauce. Season to taste with salt and pepper, adding the Tabasco sauce, if using.

3 Keep the mayonnaise cold until ready to serve, then spoon over the hot salmon.

teriyaki salmon
on **noodles**

4 skinless salmon fillets, weighing about 4 oz/125 g each

2 tablespoons soy sauce

1 tablespoon dry sherry

2 tablespoons soft brown sugar

2 garlic cloves, crushed

1 teaspoon grated fresh ginger root

1 tablespoon sesame oil

2 tablespoons water

2 tablespoons sesame seeds

2 scallions, chopped

8 oz/250 g dried rice noodles, cooked according to the instructions on the package

3 tablespoons chopped cilantro leaves

1 Place the salmon on a foil-lined broiler pan. Mix together the soy sauce, sherry, sugar, garlic, ginger root, half of the oil, and the water. Brush half of the marinade over the salmon and set aside for 10 minutes.

2 Cook the salmon under a preheated hot broiler for 5–6 minutes, turning it halfway through the cooking time and brushing with a little more of the marinade.

3 Meanwhile, heat the remaining oil in a saucepan, add the sesame seeds and scallions, and fry for 1 minute.

4 Add the noodles and any remaining marinade to the saucepan and heat through. Stir in the cilantro. Serve the salmon on a bed of noodles.

chargrilled **mustard salmon** with **lime zucchini**

4 salmon fillets, weighing about 7 oz/200 g each

1 tablespoon prepared English mustard

1 teaspoon grated fresh ginger root

1 teaspoon crushed garlic

2 teaspoons honey

1 tablespoon light soy sauce or tamari sauce

Lime Zucchini

2 tablespoons olive oil

1 lb/500 g zucchini, thinly sliced lengthways

grated zest and juice of 1 lime

2 tablespoons chopped mint

salt and pepper

1 Place the salmon fillets, skin-side down, in a shallow flameproof dish. They should fit snugly in a single layer. Mix the mustard, ginger, garlic, honey, and soy sauce or tamari, then spoon this mixture evenly over the fillets. Season to taste with salt and pepper and set aside.

2 To cook the lime zucchini, heat the olive oil in a large nonstick skillet. Add the zucchini and fry, stirring often, for 5–6 minutes, or until they are lightly browned and tender. Stir in the lime zest and juice and the mint and season with salt and pepper. Remove from the heat and keep hot.

3 While the zucchini are cooking, heat the broiler on the hottest setting. Broil the salmon fillets for 10–15 minutes, depending on their thickness, until lightly charred on top and cooked through. Serve hot, with the lime zucchini.

griddled salmon fillets
with **pesto** and **lemon rice**

⅓ cup/75 g long-grain rice

grated zest and juice of 1 lemon

4 salmon fillets, weighing
    5 oz/150 g each

¼ cup/50 g butter

basil leaves, to garnish (optional)

Pesto

1 garlic clove, chopped

6 tablespoons/15 g basil leaves

1 tablespoon/15 g pine nuts

3 tablespoons extra virgin olive oil

1 tablespoon freshly grated
    Parmesan cheese

sea salt flakes and pepper

1 Bring a large saucepan of water to a boil, add the rice and the lemon zest, and return to a boil. Simmer gently for 10–12 minutes until the rice is cooked. Meanwhile, to make the pesto, place all the ingredients in a food processor or blender and process until smooth or use a mortar and pestle.

2 Heat a griddle pan. Remove any bones from the salmon with tweezers and pat the salmon dry with paper towel. Place the fillets on the hot griddle, skin-side down, and cook for 3 minutes. Turn them over and cook for another 2–3 minutes until cooked through and firm to the touch.

3 Drain the rice and immediately stir in the lemon juice and butter. Season to taste with salt and pepper. Serve the salmon fillets on a bed of rice with the pesto sauce. Garnish with basil leaves, if liked.

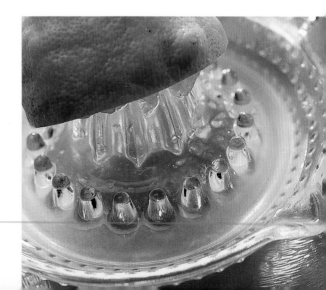

griddled salmon with sour cream and mock caviar

4 salmon fillets, weighing
  5 oz/150 g each, skinned

⅔ cup/150 ml sour cream

3½ oz/100 g black and/or red fish
  eggs

pepper

chopped scallions

griddled lemon wedges, to serve

Fish eggs come in a variety of sizes and colors. The most widely available are lumpfish roe that have been salted, colored black or red, and pressed. The name red caviar is sometimes used for salmon eggs.

1 Heat a griddle pan. Place the salmon fillets on the griddle and cook for 4–5 minutes on each side.

2 Arrange the salmon on 4 individual plates and spoon sour cream on top. Top with fish eggs and chopped scallions, and season with black pepper. Serve with griddled lemon wedges.

sesame-crusted
salmon fillet salad

1 lb/500 g salmon fillet

2 egg whites, lightly beaten

1 tablespoon white sesame seeds

1 tablespoon black sesame seeds

2 bunches of watercress

1 curly endive, divided into leaves

4 scallions, cut into thin strips and
placed in water

salt and pepper

Dressing

3 tablespoons white wine vinegar

5 tablespoons vegetable oil

1 tablespoon soy sauce

1 tablespoon sesame oil

1 teaspoon sugar

1 bunch of chives, chopped

1 Dip the salmon in the egg white. Mix the white and black sesame seeds with salt and pepper on a large plate. Roll the salmon in the sesame seeds and pat on the seeds all over to give a good even coating. Heat a griddle pan, place the salmon on it, and cook for 2 minutes on each side for rare, or 5 minutes for well done.

2 Put all the dressing ingredients in a food processor or blender and mix thoroughly. Toss the watercress and endive in the dressing and arrange on a large serving dish.

3 Slice the salmon fillet with a sharp, thin-bladed knife and arrange on top of the salad. Drain the scallion curls, dry them on paper towels, and sprinkle over the salmon.

puy lentils
with **flaked salmon** and **dill**

1-lb/500-g salmon tail fillet

2 tablespoons dry white wine

4 red bell peppers, halved, cored, and seeded

2 cups/175 g Puy lentils, well rinsed

large handful of dill, chopped

1 bunch of scallions, finely sliced

lemon juice, for squeezing

pepper

Dressing

2 garlic cloves

large handful of flat-leaf parsley, chopped

large handful of dill, chopped

1 teaspoon Dijon-style mustard

2 green chilies, seeded and chopped

juice of 2 large lemons

1 tablespoon extra virgin olive oil

1 Place the salmon on a sheet of foil and spoon over the wine. Gather up the foil and fold over at the top to seal. Place on a cookie sheet and bake in a preheated oven at 400°F for 15–20 minutes until cooked. Allow to cool, then flake, cover, and chill.

2 Flatten the bell pepper halves slightly. Broil skin-side up under a preheated hot broiler until charred. Enclose in a plastic bag for a few minutes. Remove from the bag, peel away the skin, and cut the flesh into 1-inch/2.5-cm cubes, reserving any juices.

3 Place all the dressing ingredients, except the oil, in a food processor or blender and process until smooth. While processing, drizzle in the oil until the mixture is thick.

4 Place the lentils in a large saucepan with plenty of water, bring to a boil, then simmer gently for about 15–20 minutes until cooked but still firm to the bite. Drain and place in a bowl with the red bell peppers, dill, and most of the scallions. Season with pepper to taste.

5 Stir the dressing into the hot lentils and allow to infuse. To serve, top the lentils with the flaked salmon and gently mix through the lentils and dressing. Squeeze over a little lemon juice and scatter with the remaining scallions.

poached fish in miso

1⅔ cups/250 g Thai fragrant rice

1⅔ cups/400 ml Fish Stock (see page 18)

1 tablespoon dark soy sauce

1 tablespoon mirin

½ tablespoon brown rice vinegar

½ tablespoon barley miso

1–2 star anise

1 tablespoon sunflower oil

4 salmon fillets, weighing about 5 oz/150 g each

2 teaspoons black onion seeds (kalonji)

salt and pepper

steamed Chinese cabbage, to serve

Miso, sometimes called bean paste, is made from fermented soybeans and is used a great deal in Japanese cooking both as a flavoring and as a condiment. It is very salty.

1 Cook the rice according to the instructions on the package and keep warm.

2 Put the stock, soy sauce, mirin, vinegar, miso, and star anise into a saucepan and bring to a boil, then cover and simmer for 5 minutes.

3 Heat the oil in a skillet and sear the salmon fillets for 1 minute on each side. Transfer the salmon to the stock, then remove the pan from the heat, but leave the salmon to poach in the hot stock for 1 minute.

4 Stir the onion seeds into the cooked rice and spoon the rice into soup plates. Top with steamed Chinese cabbage and poached salmon and pour in the stock.

salmon steaks
with **oriental sauce**
and **noodles**

4 salmon steaks or fillets, weighing about 6 oz/175 g each

7 oz/200 g dried Chinese noodles

1 chili, finely chopped

1 bunch of scallions, cut into long thin strips

1 bunch of cilantro, roughly chopped

2 tablespoons sesame oil

Oriental Sauce

4 tablespoons teriyaki sauce

4 tablespoons oyster sauce

4 tablespoons hoisin sauce

½ teaspoon Tabasco sauce

To garnish
griddled chilies
cilantro sprigs

1 Heat a griddle pan. Place the salmon steaks or fillets on the griddle and cook for 4 minutes on each side.

2 Meanwhile, make the oriental sauce. Mix together the teriyaki, oyster, hoisin, and Tabasco sauces in a small saucepan and heat through gently.

3 Cook the noodles in a large saucepan of lightly salted boiling water for 3 minutes. Drain well.

4 Add the chopped chili, scallions, chopped cilantro, and sesame oil to the noodles and toss together thoroughly. Arrange the noodles and griddled salmon on individual plates and garnish with griddled chilies and cilantro sprigs. Serve the oriental sauce separately.

salmon and zucchini brochettes

salmon fillet weighing about
1½–2 lb/750g–1 kg, skinned and
cut into ½-inch/1-cm cubes

12 oz/375 g zucchini, cut into
½-inch/1-cm pieces

Marinade

8 tablespoons sunflower oil

2 tablespoons light sesame seed oil

2 tablespoons sesame seeds

1 garlic clove, crushed

1–2 tablespoons lime juice

pepper

To serve

arugula

whole chives

lime wedges

These brochettes can also be made with fresh tuna or swordfish. Mashed potatoes flavored with olive oil go very well with them. If you are using wooden skewers soak them in cold water for 30 minutes first so that they do not burn.

1 First prepare the marinade. Put all the ingredients into a large bowl and whisk together. Add the salmon and zucchini pieces and toss to coat them thoroughly. Cover the bowl and leave the salmon to marinate for about 30 minutes.

2 Thread the salmon and zucchini pieces alternately onto the skewers and cook the brochettes under a preheated very hot broiler or over a hot barbecue for about 5 minutes, turning them frequently and brushing with the marinade to keep the fish and zucchini from drying out. The fish is cooked when it is just beginning to look milky. Take care not to overcook it or it will become dry and tough. Serve immediately on a bed of arugula and garnish with whole chives and lime wedges.

4 Simple Suppers

double-decker salmon

4 salmon steaks, weighing about 7 oz/200 g each, cut toward the tail end

1 cup/50 g fresh white breadcrumbs

3 oz/75 g sun-dried tomatoes in oil, drained and roughly chopped

3 tablespoons olive oil (from a jar of sun-dried tomatoes)

3 tablespoons chopped mint

1¼ cups/125 g feta cheese, drained and crumbled

salt and pepper

1 Arrange the salmon steaks on a cookie sheet.

2 Put the breadcrumbs, sun-dried tomatoes, oil, and mint into a bowl. Crumble in the feta cheese, add salt and pepper to taste, and mix thoroughly. Divide the breadcrumb mixture among the salmon pieces and press it down firmly on the salmon with the back of the spoon to keep it in place.

3 Cook the salmon in a preheated oven at 375°F for 20 minutes until the fish flakes when pressed with a knife. Transfer to serving plates and serve either on a bed of cooked, sliced new potatoes or lemon-flavored couscous flecked with chopped watercress.

broiled salmon
with mashed celeriac

1⅔ cups/250 g celeriac, diced

1¼ cups/300 g canned cannellini
   beans, drained and rinsed

juice of 1 lemon

2 tablespoons snipped chives

pinch of grated nutmeg

2 salmon steaks, weighing about
   5 oz/150 g each

2 teaspoons olive oil

4 cups/125 g baby spinach, stems
   removed

2 teaspoons balsamic vinegar

salt and pepper

chives, to garnish (optional)

This unusual fish supper is quick and easy to put together.

1 Cook the celeriac in a saucepan of boiling water for 15 minutes, until just tender. Drain the beans and mash with the lemon juice, chopped chives, nutmeg, and salt and pepper.

2 While the celeriac is cooking, put the salmon steaks on a broiler pan, drizzle with the oil, and season to taste with salt and pepper. Cook the salmon under a preheated broiler, placing the rack 2 inches/5 cm away from the heat, for 5 minutes. Turn the salmon over and cook the other side for a further 2 minutes, or until the fish flakes when pressed with a knife.

3 Meanwhile, steam the spinach for 2 minutes, until just wilted. Reheat the mashed celeriac and beans, if necessary, spoon onto plates, and top with the spinach. Remove the skin from the salmon and place it skinned-side down on the spinach. Drizzle with balsamic vinegar and garnish with extra chives, if using.

salmon with pesto and pasta

3⅔ cups/325 g dried penne

2 tablespoons olive oil

1 onion, thinly sliced

13-oz/400-g can red or pink salmon

1 cup/150 g frozen peas

2 tablespoons pesto

1 tablespoon lemon juice

¼ cup/25 g Parmesan cheese, freshly grated

salt and pepper

Parmesan shavings, to garnish

Canned salmon might not taste as good as its fresh counterpart, but it's ideal for creating an easy meal in minutes. Bottled pesto sauce is another valuable storecupboard standby. For this recipe, use either the familiar green pesto, made from basil and Parmesan, or the lesser-known red pesto—flavored with bell peppers and tomatoes.

1 Cook the pasta in plenty of lightly salted boiling water for about 8–10 minutes until almost tender.

2 Meanwhile, heat the oil in a skillet, add the onion, and fry for about 5 minutes until softened. Drain the salmon and discard any skin and bones. Roughly flake the flesh with a fork.

3 Add the peas to the pasta and cook for a further 3 minutes. Drain the pasta and peas, retaining a few tablespoons of the cooking water, and return to the pan.

4 Stir in the pesto, lemon juice, Parmesan, onion, water, and flaked salmon. Season lightly with salt and pepper and toss gently. Serve immediately, topped with Parmesan shavings and accompanied by a leafy salad, if liked.

creamy **salmon kedgeree**

¼ **cup/50 g butter**

1 **large onion, finely chopped**

1 **cup/175 g long-grain rice, cooked until just tender**

1 **lb/500 g cooked salmon, broken into large flakes and bones removed**

3 **hard-cooked eggs, roughly chopped**

2 **tablespoons finely chopped parsley**

⅔ **cup/150 ml light cream**

salt and pepper

1 **tablespoon finely chopped chives, to garnish**

1 Melt half the butter in a large skillet and fry the onion until soft. Stir in the rice and season well with salt and pepper.

2 Add the salmon, eggs, parsley, and cream, folding them carefully into the rice to prevent the fish and eggs from breaking up too much.

3 Pile the kedgeree into an ovenproof dish, cover with buttered foil, and heat through in a preheated oven at 350°F for 15 minutes. When hot, serve sprinkled with the chopped chives.

SERVES: 2 PREPARATION TIME: 30 minutes
COOKING TIME: about 45 minutes

creamy **fish pie**

4 small baking potatoes, (weighing about 500 g in total), cut into large chunks

1 small leek, diced

1 salmon steak, weighing about 8 oz/250 g

1 cod steak, weighing about 7 oz/200 g

1¼ cups/300 ml skim milk

¼ cup/50 g butter

3 tablespoons/25 g all-purpose flour

grated zest and juice of ½ lemon

2 tablespoons chopped parsley, plus extra to garnish

salt and pepper

This light and creamy salmon and cod pie, topped with a delicious lemon and leek mash, can be made early in the day and then reheated when needed.

1 Cook the potatoes in lightly salted boiling water for 15 minutes until tender. Steam the leek for 4–5 minutes until tender.

2 Meanwhile, put the salmon and cod into a saucepan with the milk. Bring to a boil, reduce the heat, and simmer for 5 minutes. Remove the pan from the heat and leave to cool for a few minutes.

3 Lift the fish out of the milk, peel away the skin, and flake the fish into large pieces. Check for any bones, then set aside, reserving the milk

4 Melt half the butter and stir in the flour. Gradually add the milk and bring to a boil, stirring until thickened and smooth. Add the lemon zest and parsley and season with salt and pepper, then carefully stir in the flaked fish. Spoon the fish mixture into a 1½-pint/900-ml shallow baking dish.

5 Drain and mash the potatoes, then beat in the leek, lemon juice, and salt and pepper. Spoon the mash over the fish mixture, fluff up the top with a fork and dot with the remaining butter. Cover loosely with plastic wrap and leave to cool, then chill until ready to cook.

6 To finish, remove the plastic wrap, stand the pie on a cookie sheet, and cook in a preheated oven at 400°F for 25 minutes until the top is golden. Garnish with extra parsley and serve.

salmon and spinach frittata

1⅔ cups/250 g new potatoes, quartered

8 oz/250 g cooked salmon

2 tablespoons olive oil

1 onion, sliced

2½ cups/75 g baby spinach

5 eggs, beaten

salt and pepper

1 tablespoon/15 g butter

1 Cook the potatoes in lightly salted boiling water for 10 minutes until just tender, then drain thoroughly. Break the fish into flakes using a knife and fork, discarding any skin and bones.

2 Heat the oil in large skillet, add the onion, and fry for 5 minutes until softened. Add the potatoes and fry for 5 minutes, stirring until lightly browned. Add the spinach and salmon and cook for 2 minutes until the spinach has just wilted and the salmon is hot.

3 Beat the eggs with the salt and pepper. Add the butter to the skillet and when it has melted pour in the eggs. Cook over a moderate heat until the eggs are almost set and the underside of the egg mixture is browned. Transfer the skillet to a preheated broiler and cook the top for 3–4 minutes until browned. Cut into wedges and serve with broiled cherry tomatoes drizzled with balsamic vinegar.

salmon sticks
with **basil** and **tomato sauce**

1-lb 6-oz/700-g salmon fillet, skinned
2 eggs
1⅔ cups/75 g fresh breadcrumbs
3 tablespoons freshly grated
    Parmesan cheese
salt and pepper

Basil and Tomato Sauce
1 tablespoon olive oil
1 onion, finely chopped
1–2 garlic cloves, chopped
13-oz/400-g can chopped tomatoes
1 teaspoon sugar
1 small bunch of basil

To finish
2 tablespoons olive oil
2 tablespoons/25 g butter
shredded basil leaves
lemon wedges

1 Cut the salmon fillet into thin slices ½ inch/1 cm wide.

2 Beat the eggs with a little salt and pepper in a shallow bowl. Mix the breadcrumbs and Parmesan cheese on a plate. Dip both sides of each salmon slice, first in the beaten egg then into the breadcrumb mixture and arrange on a cookie sheet. Chill until ready to cook.

3 To make the sauce, heat the oil in a small saucepan, add the onion and garlic, and fry for 5 minutes, stirring until softened. Stir in the canned tomatoes, sugar, and a little salt and pepper. Simmer for 5 minutes, stirring occasionally, until thickened. Chop some of the basil to give about 2 tablespoons, then stir it into the sauce. Remove the pan from the heat and keep warm.

4 When you are ready to serve, heat half the remaining oil and butter in a skillet, add as many fish strips as will fit comfortably into it, and fry for 5 minutes, turning once or twice until golden. Lift them out of skillet, drain on paper towels, and fry the remaining salmon in the same way with rest of the oil and butter. Divide the salmon sticks among the serving plates, garnish with a few torn basil leaves, and serve with lemon wedges. Reheat the sauce and serve separately in a bowl.

salmon **fish cakes** with **spinach** and **poached egg**

8 oz/250 g round red or round white
  potatoes, quartered

10-oz/300-g salmon fillet, skinned
  and bones removed

1–2 tablespoons all-purpose flour

6–8 tablespoons sunflower or
  groundnut oil

1 lb/500 g spinach

4 medium eggs

salt and pepper

lemon wedges, to serve

Salmon fish cakes are some of the finest, and quick to make and cook. If you particularly like raw salmon and have a very fresh piece of salmon fillet, you can make a delicious raw fish cake—a salmon tartare of finely chopped fillet topped with tiny capers and finely chopped hard-cooked egg and parsley.

1 Cook the potatoes in lightly salted boiling water until they are just tender when pierced with a sharp knife. Drain well and leave to cool.

2 Either roughly chop the salmon or ground it briefly in a food processor to a coarse consistency. Using a fork or the back of a wooden spoon, roughly mash the potatoes with salt and pepper. Add the ground salmon and mix together.

3 With floured hands, divide the mixture into 4 pieces and press firmly into 4 plump fish cakes. Coat each fish cake in flour and chill for 1 hour.

4 Pour the oil into a large skillet and heat until hot. Add the fish cakes and cook for 3–4 minutes on each side.

5 Shake the washed spinach leaves dry, pack them into a saucepan, and cover with a lid. Heat gently for 2–3 minutes, or until the spinach has just begun to wilt. Drain the spinach thoroughly and season with a little salt and pepper.

6 Poach the eggs until just cooked. Remove the fish cakes from the oil and set them on individual plates, top each one with some of the spinach, and finish with a hot poached egg. Serve with lemon wedges.

salmon in **puff pastry**

2 lb/1kg salmon, skinned and filleted

2 tablespoons/25 g butter

2 strips of rindless fatty bacon, chopped

1½ cups/125 g mushrooms, chopped

½ cup/125 g soft cheese with garlic and herbs

2 tablespoons milk

1 lb/500 g puff pastry, defrosted if frozen

beaten egg, to glaze

salt and pepper

1 Season the salmon fillets on both sides. Melt the butter in a skillet, add the bacon, and fry for about 5 minutes, until crisp. Add the mushrooms and sauté for about 2 minutes until softened, stirring all the time. Stir in the soft cheese and milk with salt and pepper to taste. Cook gently, stirring until well mixed. Remove from the heat and leave to cool.

2 Roll out half the pastry to measure 1 inch/2.5 cm larger all around than the reassembled fish. Transfer the pastry to a greased baking pan and place one fish fillet, skinned-side down, in the center. Spread with the cheese mixture and cover with the second salmon fillet, skinned-side up.

3 Brush the edges of the pastry with a little of the egg. Roll out the remaining pastry and cover the fish. Trim the edges, then pinch them together to seal. Roll out the pastry trimmings and cut them into strips. Brush the top of the pie with beaten egg and arrange the strips in a lattice design over the top. Brush again with beaten egg.

4 Bake the pie in a preheated oven 400°F for 35–40 minutes, until the pastry is crisp and golden brown. Serve hot with asparagus or zucchini, or cold with a salad.

salmon and red bell pepper pie

2 tablespoons olive oil

2 red bell peppers, cored, seeded, and chopped

2 eggs

8-oz/250-g salmon fillet, skinned and cubed

1 zucchini, sliced

1 teaspoon chopped dill

Pastry

3 cups/375 g all-purpose flour

1½ cups/175 g chilled butter, diced

2 egg yolks

salt and pepper

beaten egg or milk, to glaze

1 To make the filling, heat the oil in a saucepan. Add the peppers, with salt and pepper to taste. Cook gently for about 10 minutes, until softened. Puree in a food processor or blender. Alternatively, press the peppers through a sieve into a bowl.

2 Meanwhile, hard-cook the eggs for 10 minutes, then drain, cool quickly, and remove the shells. Chop the eggs and add to the pepper puree with the salmon, zucchini, and dill. Mix well.

3 To make the pastry, place the flour in a bowl with ½ teaspoon salt. Cut in the butter with a pastry blender until the mixture resembles fine breadcrumbs. Add the egg yolks with enough cold water, about 3–4 tablespoons, to mix to a firm dough.

4 Turn the dough out on a lightly floured surface and knead briefly. Roll out just over half and line a 9 x 1½-inch/23 x 3-cm pie plate. Fill with the salmon mixture and dampen the edges of the pastry with water.

5 Roll out the remaining pastry and cover the pie. Pinch the edges to seal, then crimp the edges to garnish. Reroll the pastry trimmings and cut them into fish tails or leaf shapes to garnish the pie. Attach the shapes with a little of the beaten egg or milk, then brush more egg or milk over the pie to glaze.

6 Bake the pie in a preheated oven at 400°F for 35–40 minutes, until the pastry is crisp and golden brown. Serve hot.

herb-crusted pink salmon

4 salmon fillets, 5 oz/150 g each, skinned

2 shallots, finely chopped

1 large bunch of dill, roughly chopped

3 tablespoons all-purpose flour

1 egg white

salt and pepper

1 Pat the salmon fillets dry with paper towels. Mix together the finely chopped shallots and the dill in a dish and season. Shake the flour onto a large plate and tip the egg white into a dish. Whisk the egg white lightly.

2 Heat a griddle pan. Dip the salmon fillets in the flour and coat them well all over. Next, dip the salmon in the egg white, again coating the fillets all over. Finally, dip the salmon in the shallot and dill mix, patting the mixture onto the fish to give it an even coating.

3 Place the salmon fillets on the griddle and cook for 4–5 minutes on each side, using a metal spatula to turn the fillets over. Serve at once with creamy mashed potatoes.

smoked salmon risotto
with **dill** and **crème fraîche**

3½ oz/100 g smoked salmon

1 cup/100 g snow peas

¼ cup/50 g butter

3 shallots, finely chopped

2 cups/375 g risotto rice

4 cups/1.2 liters hot Fish Stock (see
 page 18)

⅔ cups/150 ml crème fraîche

4 tablespoons chopped dill

salt and pepper

1 Cut the salmon into small pieces. Slice the snow peas lengthways into thin slices.

2 Melt the butter in a large, heavy saucepan. Sauté the shallots for 5 minutes until soft but not colored. Add the rice and stir well to coat the grains with the butter.

3 Add the hot stock, a large ladleful at a time, stirring until each addition is absorbed into the rice. Continue adding stock in this way, cooking until the rice is creamy but the grains are still firm. This should take about 20 minutes.

4 Add the smoked salmon, shredded snow peas, and half the crème fraîche and dill, stirring gently for about 1 minute, until the salmon has turned opaque. Season to taste with salt and pepper. Cover and leave the risotto to rest for a few minutes, then spoon over the remaining crème fraîche, if liked, and serve scattered with the remaining dill.

5 Something Special

bourride

2 tablespoons olive oil

1 onion, roughly chopped

1 fennel bulb, core discarded, quartered, and sliced,

1 zucchini, diced

1 red or orange bell pepper, cored, seeded, and sliced

2 garlic cloves, chopped

1 lb/500 g tomatoes, skinned and chopped

1¼ cups/300 ml Fish Stock (see page 18)

1 cup/200 ml white wine or extra stock

2 large pinches saffron threads

4 teaspoons tomato paste

2 teaspoons sugar

4 salmon steaks, weighing about 7 oz/200 g each

salt and pepper

torn basil leaves or flat-leaf parsley, to garnish

French bread, to serve

1 Heat the oil in a deep skillet with a lid or a large saucepan. Add the onion and fry for 5 minutes, stirring until softened and lightly browned. Add the fennel, zucchini, pepper, and garlic and fry for 2 minutes.

2 Stir in the chopped tomatoes, fish stock, wine, if using, saffron, tomato paste, and sugar, and season with salt and pepper. Bring to a boil, stirring.

3 Put the salmon steaks in the skillet in a single layer and spoon some of the sauce and vegetables over them. Cover and cook gently for 10 minutes. Turn the fish over and cook for 2–4 minutes, or until it flakes when lightly pressed with a knife.

4 Spoon the salmon, vegetables, and sauce into shallow serving bowls, leaving the fish whole or breaking it into large chunks and discarding the skin and bones if preferred. Sprinkle with torn herb leaves and serve with French bread.

sole and smoked salmon paupiettes

6 skinned sole fillets, weighing about 2 oz/50 g each

3 slices smoked salmon, weighing about 1 oz/25 g each

1 tablespoon chopped dill

1¼ cups/300 ml Fish Stock (see page 18)

2 oz/50 g cooked shelled shrimp

salt and pepper

Herb and Lemon Sauce

2 hard-cooked egg yolks

grated zest and juice of 1 lemon

1 teaspoon French-style mustard

1 teaspoon soft dark brown sugar

4 tablespoons Fish Stock (see page 18) or vegetable stock

2 tablespoons olive oil

4 tablespoons low-fat plain yogurt

1 tablespoon each finely chopped tarragon, basil, and parsley

salt and pepper

dill sprigs, to garnish

These light paupiettes melt in the mouth.

1 Lay the sole fillets flat and season with salt and pepper. Cut the slices of smoked salmon in half lengthways and lay a strip down the length of each sole fillet. Sprinkle with chopped dill and roll up loosely. Secure with wooden toothpicks.

2 Place the fish rolls in a shallow pan and add the fish stock. It should cover the fish. Cover and simmer for about 8 minutes until just tender. Drain the fish and keep warm on a serving dish.

3 Meanwhile, make the herb and lemon sauce. Mix the hard-cooked egg yolks to a paste with the lemon zest and juice, mustard, and sugar. Gradually beat in the stock, olive oil, and yogurt. Add the herbs and salt and pepper to taste.

4 Spoon 4 tablespoons of the fish cooking liquid into a small pan and boil quickly over a high heat until reduced to about 1 tablespoon.

5 Stir the herb and lemon sauce and the shrimp into the reduced cooking liquid and heat through gently. Spoon the sauce evenly over the fish paupiettes and garnish with dill sprigs.

celebration baked salmon

4-lb 13-oz/2.4-kg whole salmon,
    well washed

1 lemon, sliced

1 small onion, sliced

1 bunch of fresh herbs

⅔ cup/150 ml dry white wine

1 cucumber, thinly sliced

melted butter (optional)

salt and pepper

mixed herbs, to garnish

Lemon Mayonnaise

grated zest of 2 lemons

13-oz/400-g jar ready-made
    mayonnaise

When serving a whole salmon cold, some people prefer to poach it rather than bake it. See page 140 for a poached salmon recipe.

1 Weigh the salmon. Line your largest roasting pan with wide foil and put the salmon on top, curving it to fit if needed. Season the inside of the body cavity, then add the lemon, onion, and herbs, sprinkling some over the top of the fish too. Pour over the wine, wrap the foil over the salmon, and seal the edges together.

2 Bake the salmon in a preheated oven at 150°F for 20 minutes per 1 lb/500 g gutted weight, or 15 minutes per 1 lb/500 g if under 4 lb/2 kg. At the end of calculated time, check that the salmon is cooked by unwrapping the foil and pressing the salmon in the center of the body cavity; the fish should flake easily and the flakes be an even color. Leave to cool.

3 Unwrap the salmon and discard the lemon, onion, and herbs. Lift the salmon onto a cutting board and strain the wine into a jug. Run a knife down the backbone of the salmon and loosen the skin at the tail end. Carefully peel away the skin, working up to the head, discarding the fins and leaving the head in place. Carefully turn the salmon over and repeat. Transfer to a large plate or tray.

4 Beginning from the tail, arrange the slices of cucumber over the salmon to look like fish scales, overlapping slightly. If liked, brush melted butter over the salmon to hold the cucumber in place. When set, cover loosely with plastic wrap and chill for up to 24 hours, or until required.

5 Stir the lemon zest into the mayonnaise and season with salt and pepper. Spoon into a serving bowl. Garnish the salmon with mixed herb sprigs just before serving.

roast fillet of salmon with saffron cream sauce

4 salmon fillets, weighing about 5–6 oz/150–175 g each

oil, for frying and roasting

salt and pepper

1–2 tablespoons finely snipped chives, to garnish

Saffron Cream Sauce

⅔ cup/150 ml Fish Stock (see page 18)

⅔ cup/150 ml dry white wine

4 saffron threads

⅔ cup/150 ml light cream

1 Season the salmon with salt and pepper. Heat a little oil in a large skillet until hot and place the salmon in the pan flesh-side down. Cook for about 2 minutes over a high heat to brown. Transfer the salmon to a lightly oiled cookie sheet, skin-side down. Season with salt and pepper and finish cooking in a preheated oven at 475°F for about 7–9 minutes, depending on the thickness of the fillet. The flesh should be opaque pink when cooked.

2 While the fish is roasting, make the sauce by combining the stock, wine, and saffron in a saucepan. Bring to a boil, then lower the heat and simmer until reduced by half. Add the cream, bring back to a boil, and boil continuously until the sauce thickens and coats the back of a spoon.

3 Serve the fish in the center of a large plate with the sauce poured around and garnished with chives. Accompany with steamed seasonal vegetables and boiled new potatoes.

SERVES: 4 PREPARATION TIME: 25 minutes, plus marinating
COOKING TIME: 8–10 minutes

griddled salmon
and **scallop salad**

1 lb/500 g salmon steak
1 lb/500 g shelled large scallops

Marinade
½ cup/125 ml light olive oil
pared zest of ½ lemon
2 teaspoons chopped oregano
1 tablespoon chopped dill
salt and pepper

Dressing
8 tablespoons Mayonnaise
   (see page 20)
4 tablespoons plain yogurt

To serve
About 4 cups/175 g mixed lettuce
   leaves (such as curly endive, red
   loose leaf, romaine, corn salad,
   arugula, or watercress)
2 cups/175 g pasta shells (optional)

Cubes of succulent salmon and scallops are threaded onto skewers for easy broiling for this salad. Serve simply on crisp leaves or add some cooked pasta shells for a more substantial dish. The seafood is good either hot or cold.

1 Mix together all the marinade ingredients and pour into a shallow dish, large enough to hold the fish.

2 Cut the salmon into chunks the same size as the scallops. Thread the salmon and scallops alternately onto 4 long skewers. Place the skewers in the marinade, turning them to coat in the flavored oil. Leave for 1½–2 hours, turning occasionally.

3 Remove the skewers from the marinade, reserving the marinade, and arrange in one layer on a broiler pan.

4 Cook the skewers under a preheated hot broiler for about 8–10 minutes, turning frequently and basting with the reserved marinade.

5 Meanwhile, stir together the mayonnaise and yogurt in a small bowl. Set aside. If using, cook the pasta according to the instructions on the package. Arrange a bed of mixed lettuce leaves with the pasta shells, if using, on 4 serving plates. To serve, remove the hot or cooled seafood from the skewers and pile onto the salad. Serve the dressing separately.

open **sushi**

4 oz/125 g sushi rice
1½ tablespoons rice wine vinegar
1 tablespoon sugar
1 teaspoon salt
4 sheets toasted nori seaweed
2-oz/50-g salmon fillet
1–2 tablespoons wasabi
a little salmon caviar
pickled ginger (optional)
soy sauce, for dipping

Wasabi is a fiercely hot, green Japanese horseradish. It is available as a paste or a powder to which water is added.

1 Cook the rice according to the instructions on the package. Immediately stir in the vinegar, sugar, and salt. Transfer the rice to a bowl set in ice and allow to cool for 10 minutes.

2 Divide the rice into 24 equal portions and with wetted hands shape into ovals. Meanwhile, cut each nori sheet into six equal strips, to make 24 in total. Cut the salmon into small dice.

3 Wrap each portion of rice with a strip of nori and seal with a dot of wasabi. Top half the sushi with the diced salmon and half with the salmon caviar. Place a single salmon egg on the diced salmon sushi.

4 Arrange the sushi on a large platter and serve with bowls of pickled ginger and soy sauce, if using, for dipping.

baked salmon in a salt crust with red bell pepper and anchovy sauce

4-lb 13-oz/2.4-kg whole salmon, well washed

18 lb/9 kg table salt

1 lemon, sliced

a few rosemary sprigs

3 tablespoons water

extra rosemary sprigs, to garnish

Red Bell Pepper and Anchovy Sauce

3 red bell peppers, cored, seeded, and quartered

4 garlic cloves, unpeeled

2 rosemary sprigs

2 tablespoons olive oil

2-oz/50-g can anchovy fillets, drained (optional)

1¼ cups/300 ml crème fraîche

If you have a combined oven and broiler, then broil the bell peppers before baking the salmon. The salt makes the salmon very heavy, so take care when lifting the pan out of the oven.

1 Weigh the salmon. Line your largest roasting pan with wide foil and pour half the salt over it. Arrange the salmon on top, curving to fit if needed. Add lemon slices and rosemary to the body cavity and close the edges with wooden satay or toothpicks.

2 Lift the foil and salt up and around the sides of the fish and pour the remaining salt over the top to cover it completely. Sprinkle with the water, then close the foil over the salt. Bake the salmon in a preheated oven at 350°F, allowing 15 minutes per 1 lb/500 g gutted weight plus 15 minutes.

3 Meanwhile, make the sauce. Put the red bell peppers, skin-side up, on a piece of foil on a broiler pan, add the garlic, and tuck the rosemary in between the bell peppers. Drizzle with the oil and broil for 10 minutes until the skins are blackened and the peppers softened. Leave to cool for 20 minutes, then peel off the skins.

4 Puree the red bell peppers, garlic, and oil in a food processor with the anchovies, if using. Stir in the crème fraîche, season with salt and pepper, and spoon into a serving bowl.

5 Peel back the foil on the salmon, crack and remove a section of the salt crust, and check that the salmon is cooked by pressing the flesh with a knife. It should flake easily and the flakes should be the same color throughout. If this is difficult, peel back a little of the skin from the top of the salmon. Lift the foil onto a serving plate, scrape off the salt, and garnish the salmon with rosemary sprigs. Serve with the red bell pepper sauce.

butterflied salmon with **juniper** and **pepper**

Juniper and Peppercorn Marinade
1½ tablespoons dried juniper berries
2 teaspoons dried green peppercorns
¼ teaspoon black peppercorns
1 teaspoon raw sugar
2–3 tablespoons oil

**4–5-lb/2–2½-kg salmon, scaled,
cleaned, boned, and butterflied
(head removed)**
a few curly endive leaves, to serve

To garnish
lemon wedges
parsley sprigs
2 scallions, finely shredded

1 First make the marinade. Coarsely grind the juniper berries and peppercorns in a spice grinder or use a mortar and pestle. Mix with the sugar and oil.

2 Open out the salmon like a book, flesh-side up, and pull out any remaining bones with tweezers. Brush over the juniper-oil marinade mixture. Close up the salmon and place it in a dish. Cover closely and marinate in the refrigerator for 2 hours.

3 About 15 minutes before cooking, remove the salmon from the refrigerator and open it up again. Place it, flesh-side up, on a baking pan. Brush it all over with any oil that has been left in the dish.

4 Place the salmon under a preheated moderate broiler, about 5–6 inches/12.5–15 cm from the source of heat and cook for 8–10 minutes, or until the flesh flakes when tested with a fork or skewer. Serve hot, with curly endive leaves, garnished with a wedge of lemon, fresh parsley, and scallions.

roasted new potatoes with smoked salmon and caviar

16 small new potatoes (weighing about 1½ oz/40 g each), scrubbed but unpeeled

2 tablespoons olive oil

1 tablespoon chopped rosemary

1 tablespoon chopped sage

½ cup/125 ml crème fraîche

4 oz/125 g smoked salmon, cut into strips

2 tablespoons lumpfish caviar

1 tablespoon snipped chives

salt and pepper

lemon wedges, to serve (optional)

This is a most delicious side dish, well worth the time spent assembling.

1 Place the potatoes in a roasting pan, add the olive oil, herbs, and some sea salt, and toss well. Put the pan on the top shelf of a preheated oven at 400°F and roast for 40–45 minutes, stirring occasionally, until the potatoes are crisp on the outside and very soft in the center.

2 Remove the potatoes from the oven and leave to cool for 5 minutes.

3 Cut a cross in the top of each potato and press it open slightly. Transfer to a serving plate and top each one with a spoonful of crème fraîche, a piece of smoked salmon, a little caviar, and snipped chives.

4 Serve immediately with plenty of pepper and lemon wedges, if liked.

whole **poached salmon** with **cold vegetables** and **aïoli**

3-lb/1.5-g salmon, scaled and gutted, washed and dried

3 quantities Court-Bouillon (see page 22)

1⅔ cups/250 g new potatoes

16–20 (about 250 g) baby carrots

18–20 5-inch asparagus spears (about 250 g)

1⅔ cups/175 g green beans

10-oz/300-g jar marinated artichoke hearts, drained

½ quantity Aïoli (see page 20)

2 tablespoons chopped basil

4 hard-cooked eggs, shelled and quartered

lemon wedges, to garnish

A fish kettle makes all the difference when poaching large fish. If you don't want to invest in one, see if you can rent one from your local catering or restaurant supplies outlet. This dish makes a stunning al fresco meal.

1 Place the salmon in a fish kettle or large heavy roasting pan and pour in the court-bouillon. Bring the liquid slowly to a boil and, as soon as it reaches a simmer, remove the pan from the heat and leave the fish in the liquid until it is completely cold.

2 Steam or boil the potatoes, carrots, asparagus, and green beans separately until tender, then refresh under running cold water. Set aside.

3 Remove the cold fish from its cooking liquid and pat dry. Carefully peel off and discard the skin and place the salmon on a large platter. Blend the aïoli and the basil and place in a bowl.

4 Arrange all the vegetables and the eggs around the salmon and serve with the basil aïoli and garnished with lemon wedges.

index

acknowledgments

All photography by **Octopus Publishing Group Ltd.**/Dave Jordan except:

Corbis UK Ltd/Richard Cummins 7

Octopus Publishing Group Ltd./Jeremy Hopeley 117/Graham Kirk 48, 133/Sandra Lane 101/William Lingwood 85/Neil Mersh 89/David Munns 1, 37/Peter Myers 2, 138/Sean Myers 81,99,121/Alan Newnham 70/William Reavell 39, 87, 95, 123/Simon Smith 15, 71/Ian Wallace 33/Philip Webb 61, 77, 93

Leigh Jones 23

Additional recipes **Sara Lewis** – Food Styling **Annie Nichols**

Executive Editor Sarah Ford
Editor Jessica Cowie
Executive Art Editor Leigh Jones
Design Tony Truscott
Production Controller Jo Sim
Picture Researcher Luzia Strohmayer